BE A
BETTER
PERSON

BE A BETTER PERSON

AN OFFERING OF SELF-REFLECTION

BC CROTHERS

Published by Atticus Publishing
548 Market Street
PMB 70756
San Francisco, CA

Library of Congress Control Number: 2023922247

ISBN: 979-8-89228-018-1   (Paperback)
ISBN: 979-8-89228-019-8   (eBook)

Printed in the United States of America

I DEDICATE THESE REFLECTIONS TO

ALL OF GOD'S PEOPLE

IN THE PRAYER

THAT THEIR LIVES

WILL CONTINUE TO REFLECT THE

EFFORT OF BRINGING

OUR FATHER'S

HEAVENLY KINGDOM

FOREVER EARTHBOUND.

TABLE OF CONTENTS
FOR REFLECTION

ACKNOWLEDGEMENTS

At a time of being puzzled as to why life's happenings are eschewed, and a few people are acting like—well, like we all will act from time to time, God sent two absolutely wonderful ladies into my circle of activity. Their spirituality, intelligence, book and life knowledge, and humor, has been a source of delight, learning, and refreshment. God is good.

Deacon Phyllis McCormick, a retired lawyer who spent her career years in New York as an advocate for the downtrodden, the underprivileged, and the mentally ill, looks quite pragmatically at life. Nothing surprises Phyllis, nothing shocks her, and she does not tell a lie, not even to save your feelings. The project facing our Deacon is the Year of Jubilee. Phyllis has vowed to raise our congregation's collective conscience by making us more aware of the problems of the earth and society. Under her astute guidance we shall become more attuned to the "what" and the "how". We are a church in for real awareness growth.

Deacon Doris Buchanan Johnson is now The Rev. Doris Buchanan Johnson, thanks be to God. On December 16, 1999, at Holy Trinity Episcopal Church in Clearwater, Florida, we celebrated the service of the Ordination of a Priest in Doris' behalf. It was a most wonderful service with plenty of laughter and tears to go around. Doris is a rare gem in that her eyes and manner blend sincerely with her words of support and encouragement. Rev. DJ has developed a technique where she is able to simultaneously nurture our "here and now" presence while gently propelling us toward the next goal, the next steppingstone experience.

As a member of the laity, it is a profound spiritual encounter and joy to serve at the altar with both these ordained Disciples of Christ. With great thanksgiving I express my appreciation and thankfulness to Doris and Phyllis as they share their love of Christ by recommending the "Scriptural Readings" found at the end of each reflection. A prayer completes the reading. Indeed, God is good.

This is the aftermath of this book's story I am not going to enjoy telling.

Confession Time: I have no idea where Deacon McCormick or The Rev. Buchanan are today. We disappeared from one another's lives over twenty years ago. I know this is a sad commentary to make on modern living, but time and distance have a way of destroying the fragility of relationships.

My prayer is that they, or someone who knows them, will make contact. This is the primary reason for the photo on the back of this book. I believe they will be pleased to see their work in print. Both ladies did a marvelous job, and were very kind to me, a budding writer.

The book's resurrection is seeing a new day. Atticus Publishing House, through the efforts of its wonderful Director, Matthew Scott, wanted this writing published as of yesterday. So, the midnight oil burned brightly, and that was all right, for God's whispers continued to be heard, just like they were all those many years ago. I thank Matthew for also hearing God-talk and Jesus-lessons in my work. It has been a very long, and sometimes painful, journey to finally find an author's home.

I also thank my best friend whose work on my behalf is without payment, and entails long, long hours fixing computer problems. Old manuscripts have formats now unknown to man and I have watched Lee Jones type, mutter, stare, and demand another cup of coffee, all the while working out another "bug". He, too, does this mighty job through the belief that these writings need to be read.

Jack, my husband, has had a particularly hard time lately. Back in April, he had an accident wherein his femur was broken. There entered pain, uncertainty, fear, and anger. There went work, paycheck, and activity. It has been difficult for Jack and me. At least, I had the writing. Jack had nursing, physical therapy, walkers, and now, a cane. Thankfully, the one thing that has not changed is Jack's willingness to help find a word or resolve a sentence structure. We work well together.

When doing spiritual direction with people, I had the occasion to point out that we will never understand why certain events happen when they do. The truthfulness of those words has come back to knock on our door.

On a happier note, I am going to close with a handwritten note I received from Susan back in the days of teaching from this book in churches.

Friday, October 27th

"Dear BC:

Thank you for letting me read this! For welcoming me into your journey and encouraging me in mine. I tend to be very skeptical of "self-improvement" projects (since I've been at this my whole life and haven't found search for perfection helpful) – but your gentle stories do wake me up! And your prayers lead me back to my only hope, to God who alone can transform me.

A particular help – your 'Desert' guided meditation on forgiveness—a way of cooperating with God.
Thanks!

Susan"

Susan knows me well enough to understand it is unto God that goes all the Glory. May you, my new group of readers, also have your soul fed with these new insights. BC

Introduction

The craving to be a better person is a personal love gift from God. It comes, though, with a price, just like God's gift of Free Will. One such price is that if we ignore this longing to be a better person, we suffer from the pangs of self-dislike, but when we respond to God's call for daily renewal, we find ourselves living a life filled with glad tidings. Surprisingly, this does not mean that bad things will not happen. Earthbound life is fraught with bad things happening to all people.

Living within a Faith-centered life means that you and I can step back and look at the occurrence through a more utilitarian lens. Our emotions and ego are not so much in play. Christian living helps us become more aware of our ignorance, realizing along the way that we are not privy to the Big Picture. We know that God operates on God's own timetable, not ours. We also trust that God's Will will be made apparent as we traverse forever forward. In striving to become our "best" and realizing that no completion "period" exists in this state of being, we single-mindedly focus on those lessons to be learned at each steppingstone experience. Eventually this results in God inviting us into the Big Picture, a vision which concentrates on righteous living now, and not hurting ourselves with instant gratification. God's invitation creates a tremendous life change.

With Divine Guidance, we will live with a desire to continually stretch beyond pettiness and frustrations. God calls us into a re-creation each day. The manner of doing this can be terribly difficult. We are to forgive. We are to let go. We are to turn aside. We are to ignore. And, importantly, we are to forget.

These are the real-life lessons our Lord gave us in His walk upon this earth. These lessons coincide with the longings found within our souls. The more we respond, listen intently, and obey, the more our souls touch God's heart.

Our life's re-creation and our soul's purification cannot be accomplished all at once. Life is lived one step at a time and our soul's endeavor for wholeness is gained inch by inch. This is why it is so important to pay attention to the little problems, the ones we like to brush off as minor annoyances. There is no such thing. In Heaven, and on Earth, all things have a unique importance. But here we run into a problem. In this life of continual busyness, we find it impossible to pay attention to all things. For this reason, we need to begin small.

"Small" is manageable. If we tend to gossip, just stopping ourselves once or twice a day from gossiping begins to water the seed of reluctance to tell tales. We notice the lack of joy and fun the next time our mouths open to spread the news of false or truth or might be. With gossip out of the picture we begin to look for other means to call people into our sphere. Maybe we learn that sparking laughter serves a higher purpose, or being acknowledged for an outstanding job brings a greater reward. Or maybe our problem is that we are too quick to judge or are too fast in speech wherein we cut off another's words. Or maybe this is backwards. Maybe we are too quick to temper and too slow to action!

Whatever our imperfections, we know that God's daily call into re-creation is a summons that requires a respondence. Initially, because we know from experience that we fail in any attempt of renewal if we bit off a piece too large. Out of necessity we begin to look for small tasks of renewal, a step-by-step process which will eventually allow our hearts, minds, and bodies to form a spiritual triad with our soul. No longer will we be at odds with our inner sanctum.

Each of this book's reflections focuses on some aspects of our lives that, to varying degrees, need improvement. I say 'our' because even though God created us as unique individuals, we certainly share similar struggles! Reading through the Holy Bible shows just how similar the human spectrum of fears, dislikes, loves, envy, and insecurities really are. As members of our Lord's family, I see how we share in the struggles for Sainthood. So, I have taken apart aspects of my own life that have had to deal with a variety of problems in the prayer that their exploration will bring about deeper awareness and thought-provoking lessons for you.

Rather than a Step One, Step Two format, the following offerings are both in the form of observations and personal reflections. With each reflection, you are encouraged to stop and think about your life. Is this an area where you could stand improvement? If so, what step could be taken that would eventually eradicate the detrimental action or response from your life? What is so striking about working on the smaller issues is that larger ones often take care of themselves in the process! This is yet another gift from God.

I have shared intimate aspects of my life with you; now you, in turn, are to share your intimacies with God. Do not feel this is unnecessary because God knows all. This is not the point. The point is that when you share with God, God shares back. From God's words, you will be directed toward the path of a deeper spiritual journey.

May God reign blessings upon your life.

THOUGHTS FROM
ATTICUS PUBLISHING

Embarking on a journey through BC Crothers's "Be a Better Person" book was like stepping into a new realm of self-awareness and spiritual enlightenment. From the very first chapter, 'Priority One', to its thought-provoking conclusion, this book guided me through a remarkable exploration of the human spirit and its capacity for growth and transformation. Her writing is infused with humility yet authoritative, making the path she lays out both challenging and reassuring.

I wholeheartedly recommend "Be a Better Person" to anyone on a quest, not just for self-improvement but for a profound, holistic transformation. It is an essential guide for anyone eager to embark on the rewarding journey of becoming their best self, infused with wisdom that only comes from deep introspection and a connection with the Divine.

Sincerely,

Matthew Scott

BE A BETTER PERSON
Reflection: Priority One

Once I paid sharp attention to only the squeaky wheel. Life was full, much too hectic for those minor annoyances seeking care. Dust bunnies gathered in corners and colorful mold cultures grew in refrigerated bowls. I discovered the value of throwing out paper, whether in the form of unanswered letters or unpaid bills. Nothing must distract that the job at hand.

Then the squeaky wheel gave way to fighting the nearest fire. Life became a series of emergencies that circled the homestead. The "ought to" and "should" gave way to the "have to". Various forms of firefighting were explored. A couple of times I shouted out the "emergency", but this method only harmed reputation. Several times I used sand in the form of paper - lots and lots of reams of paper - to extinguish a blaze. Other means included delegating or manipulating people, time, equipment, or appointments. I learned that 'patching' was quite an acceptable fire-fighting tool as it was far less time consuming. Getting to the bottom of the matter, clean slates, and done deeds in the form of *periods* were deemed as accomplishments that slowed the system. Better to move at a rapid pace, even if less is accomplished. "Less as more" received official sanction.

Then came the present day where daily life is all about whirlwinds. Everything appears to either require immediate attention or a limited time, or extreme-focused attention. Airlines, doctors, restaurants, and schedules become harried, overbooked. One-hour appointments are as obsolete as a typewriter. If you cannot say it in 15 minutes or less, then write it in a letter but no longer than one pager or, better yet, send an email.

Help! No wonder feeling out of shorts has become normal. When was the last time we mediated, or observed clouds forming pictures? When was the last time we surrounded ourselves with silence? When was the last time we meandered through the woods or sank our toes into warm sand? Or when was the last time we sequestered ourselves behind locked doors for a long, hot soak watching skin turn rosy-pink, or heard poetry read aloud, or experienced a candlelit dinner? And, more importantly, when was the last time we crawled into God and listened to our souls joyfully resonating from the awareness of being with God, in God?

Earthbound, everything and everyone around are priorities. Well, listen, you people in my life: I want to be a priority! God wants me to be a priority! The Holy Bible alone tells me this is so in countless ways. I need to stop doing the others-activity and the must-do activities, and just concentrate on being me, a be-ing. This is a spiritual priority and God's mandate! Enough with spending my days dancing to the tunes of others. If I make the all of me into a priority, while I may never find that ever-elusive period, I will, upon contemplation and relaxation, emerge a very satisfied semi-colon.

How are your semi-colons doing? Or are you still dancing for others? Want to change? Not as hard as you might think. Stretch out your hand to our Lord. You will feel Jesus's touch. Follow. You are being led to your next steppingstone.

Scriptural Readings by Johnson & McCormick

1Kings 19.9-14a "There he went into a cave and spent the night there. Then the word of Yahweh came to him saying, 'What are you doing here, Elijah?' He replied, 'I am full of jealous zeal for

Yahweh Sabaoth, because the Israelites have abandoned your covenant, have torn down your altars and put your prophets to the sword. I am the only one left, and now they want to kill me.' Then he was told, 'Go out and stand on the mountain before Yahweh.' For at that moment Yahweh was going by. A might hurricane split the mountains and shattered the rocks before Yahweh. But Yahweh was not in the hurricane. And after the hurricane, an earthquake. But Yahweh was not in the earthquake. And after the earthquake, fire. But Yahweh was not in the fire. And after the fire, a light murmuring sound. And when Elijah heard this, he covered his face with his cloak and went out and stood at the entrance of the cave. Then a voice came to him, which said, 'What are you doing here, Elijah?' He replied, 'I am full of jealous zeal for Yahweh, God Sabaoth, because the Israelites have abandoned your covenant, have tom down your altars and put your prophets to the sword."
New Jerusalem Bible

2Corinthians 4.7-10 "We are no better than pots of earthenware to contain this treasure, and this proves that such transcendent power does not come from us but is God's alone. Hard-pressed on every side, we are never hemmed in; bewildered, we are never at our wits' end; hunted, we are never abandoned to our fate; struck down, we are not left to die. Wherever we go we carry death with us in our body, the death that Jesus died, that in this body also life may reveal itself, the life that Jesus lives."
The New English Bible

Today's Prayer "Hello, God. Did I even say good morning to You? Or think of You often during the day? Will You forgive me? I am busy. Sometimes I am so busy I don't remember when I began, or where I left off. There are times I stand in the middle of the room or street or store and wonder what it was I was supposed to be doing. Today, I ran after a thought but never did quite catch it. The phone rang several times, but

I managed to ignore it. I pray it was nothing important. There are items of 'things to do' on the list that have yet to be crossed out and several have been on that list for quite a while. I'm always playing catch up, but I never do. I am tired. And tired of doing so many, many tasks that end up meaning nothing.

I think it is time for just You and I, God, don't You? You are so much a part of who I am and who I want to be. I tell my family and friends that if we are all to grow together and share our lives, then we need to spend time together; that rare 'quality' time. Yet, I don't do this with You, You who will be here long after friends and family has departed. I am going to make this change right now.

"Hello, God. How would You like to spend the next couple of minutes with me? Have I got a story for You. Listen *(your own words to be added)*. Amen, amen."

BE A BETTER PERSON
Reflection: The Gift Of Remembrance

It came through the mail, enclosed inside, of all things, a Christmas card. It is not the place you would expect to receive a death notice but there it was—a friend from the past had died. Her ashes were being sent down and the memorial service would be held next week.

Now you know how rushed the holidays are, what with shopping, decorations, gift-wrapping, parties, an Open House, additional church services, extra cooking, guests, card writing and package mailing. There is way too much to do. I am in the process of stealing a couple of hours—just for me. Now this.

A funeral right at my planned stolen time.

Listen. Her family moved away years ago. She never wrote. I heard about them from time to time via word of mouth from others in the church. She hasn't been gone long enough that I forget what she looks like, but she has been away. We were friends though. Not super close friends, but close enough to share a few life experiences and private thoughts while drinking a cup of coffee.

We had some good times. She was the one who taught me how to make angels out of cardboard, starched cotton, rug samples, and broken bits of jewelry. I later made pin money selling several of them at a craft show. She also taught me how to make clouds out of gossamer, glitter, and string for the children's play. Oh, and I remember when I sprained my ankle cooking up a batch of eggs for the Easter

Egg Hunt and she rushed me to the Free Clinic. What a hoot! Smashed egg yolk ran down my arms and legs, and a captured tiny live chick kept chirping and sticking his head out of my pocket. How she howled with laughter! The doctor thought we were nuts.

But that was a long time ago, and the latest selling hot novel and hot tub are now.

Yet, in reflection, what I remember most of all is the crisis. Her child died from Multiple Sclerosis. Nothing is worse than the death of a child. Nothing is harder to live through than a parent surviving their child. Her heart broke in two. Yet, through out it all, she carried her Faith as a shield. Not to say she became a Jesus freak or a scripture-quoting crazy person. No, she accepted strength from Grace, and pain protection from the Holy Spirit. She relied on the fact that from God she would one day have an answer as to why her child had been taken so young. And she relied on our Lord to see her through the struggle of daily sorrow. I saw her grow stronger, graceful, and gentler with others and herself. Her understanding of another's pain grew out of her own. The deficit of death she turned into a living plus by accepting what she could not change. She became quietly thoughtful and often asked God's Will before making decisions. These transitions of hers influenced me as I found myself beginning to rely more on God's daily message than my own ego.

Maybe I do have the time to go to her funeral.

Thank you, dear Lord, for the remembrance of memories.

Scriptural Readings by Johnson & McCormick

Deuteronomy 4.9 "However, take care and be earnestly on your guard not to forget the things which your own eyes have seen, nor let them slip from your memory as long as you live, but teach them to your children and to your children's children."
New American Bible

Matthew 7.12 "Therefore all things whatsoever ye would that men should do to you, do ye even so to them: for is the law and the prophets.'" King James Version

Luke 6.31 "Do to others as you would have them do to you." New Revised Standard Version

Today's Prayer "Over and over again, dear Lord, You prove that You are close at hand, every time I need You. Most times I think I need Your presence when I am afraid or in trouble or in pain, but the truth is—I need You most when I don't realize there is a need. Like with remembering. I take it very much for granted that I will remember what is important and will certainly forget what is not needed or what is harmful or hurtful. But this simply isn't so. I cannot be trusted to let go of 'bad' memories in a timely fashion or be the keeper of good ones. I need You for this. I can trust that You will always recall to my mind those lessons that need to be remembered and those that need to be acted upon. You will be my backdoor, The One who covers my oversight or neglect. My responsibility will be to respond to those memories in the way You would have me act—that is, to *do right.* With the guidance of the Holy Spirit, I will discern our Father's will and act accordingly. Yours is a Gift of Memories and I thank You for it, dear Lord. Amen."

BE A BETTER PERSON
Reflection: In The Eyes Of God

Excuse me, but Miss Cocoa is not your ordinary alley cat, though she certainly looked it at first sight. I had just walked two miles and was beginning to feel aches and cramps in feet and toes. Not in a good mood, running late, and feeling slightly stupid for the sudden burst of energy that sent me flying into a parked car, I was limping through the church courtyard on my way to choir practice when I heard this pitiful cry. At first, I thought it was an echo to my own crying thoughts about having to walk home after practice, but no, when peering onto the foyer, I spotted this black, skinny cat. It ignored me while trying to con the church cat into letting it eat out of his bowl.

"No, no, no," I told God. "No way am I taking another one home."

We already had four cats running around. They were hardly noticeable in a 3500 square-foot house so their number was tolerable but one more, I was convinced, would drown our home in cat hair and the abundant Florida fleas.

All through my tirade of telling God what I would not do, I heard the howling of the pathetic cat. She sounded so sad over her abandonment. Relenting before God's Will I said, "All right, You win. If this creature is still here when choir practice is over, I'll take it home." Convinced our church tom would chase this food thief away, I gamely climbed the steps. Never mind my attitude when arriving home later that evening, crippled with a cramped foot and a screaming cat.

For three very long days, she stayed in the kitchen where she ate, drank, used the cat box, and slept in perfect contentment. When she was convinced she would live to eat yet another meal, she let me pick her up—which I did, driving her straight to the vets. Image my surprise when he announced, "This new cat of yours is an expensive rare Havana Brown from England!" Well, didn't I look at her with new eyes—"You precious darling, you!"

It is true that we humans love what is rare, unique.

When do you think we will begin to realize that this is how God looks at each one of us?

Scriptural Readings by Johnson & McCormick

Luke 15.11-32 "He went on to say, 'A man had two sons. The younger one said to his father, 'Dad, give me my share of the business.' So he split up the business between them. Not so long after that the younger one packed up all his stuff and took off for a foreign land, where he threw his money away living like a fool. Soon he ran out of cash, and on top of that, the country was in a deep depression. So he was really hard up. He finally landed a job with one of the citizens of that country, who sent him into the fields to feed hogs! And he was hungry enough to tank up on the slop the hogs were eating. Nobody was given him even a hand-out.

"One day an idea bowled him over. 'A lot of my father's hired hands have more than enough bread to eat, and out here I'm starving in this depression. I'm gonna get up and go to my father and say, 'Dad, I've sinner against God and you, and am no longer fit to be called you son - just make me one of your hired hands.'

"So he got up and came to his father. While he was some distance down the road, his father saw him and was moved to tears. He ran to him and hugged him and kissed him and kissed him.

"The boy said, 'Dad, I've sinner against God and you, and I'm not fit to be your son any more-' But the father said to his servants, 'You all run quick and get the best suit you can find and put it on him. Get his family ring for his hand and some dress shoes for his feet. Then I want you to bring that stall-fed steer and butcher it, and let's all eat and whoop it up, because this son of mine was given up for dead, and he's still alive; he was lost and is now found." The Cotton Patch Version of Luke and Acts

Luke 19.1-9 "Jesus entered Jericho and was passing through. A man was there by the name of Zacchaeus; he was a chief tax collector and was wealthy. He wanted to see who Jesus was, but being a short man he could not, because of the crowd. So he ran ahead and climbed a sycamore-fig tree to see him since Jesus was coming that way. When Jesus reached the spot, he looked up aid said to him, 'Zacchaeus, come down immediately. I must stay at your house today.' So he came down at once and welcomed him gladly.

"All the people saw this and began to mutter, 'He has gone to be the guest of a 'sinner'.

"But Zacchaeus stood up and said to the Lord, 'Look, Lord! Here and now I give half of my possessions to the poor, and if I have cheated anybody out of anything, I will pay back four times the amount.'

"Jesus said to him, 'Today salvation has come to this house, because this man, too, is a son of Abraham. For the Son of Man came to seek and to save what was lost.'" New International Version, The Living Insights Study Bible

John 8.3-12 "The scribes and the Pharisees brought a woman who had been caught in adultery; and making her stand before all of them, they said to him, 'Teacher, this woman was caught in the very act of committing adultery. Now in the law Moses commanded us to stone such women. Now what do you say?' They said this to test him, so that they might have some charge to bring against him. Jesus bent down and wrote with his finger on the ground. When they kept on questioning him, he straightened up and said to them, 'Let anyone among you who is without sin be the first to throw a stone at her.' And once again he bent down and wrote on the ground. When they heard it, they went away, one by one, beginning with the elders; and Jesus was left alone with the woman standing before him. Jesus straightened up and said to her, Woman, where are they? Has no one condemned you?' She said, 'No one, sir.' And Jesus said, 'Neither do I condemn you. Go your way, and from now on do not sin again.'

"Again Jesus spoke to them, saying, 'I am the light of the world. Whoever follows me will never walk in darkness but will have the light of life.'" New Revised Standard Version

Today's Prayer "Father, with repentant heart, I cannot think of one sin I have ever brought before You that You withheld Your forgiveness. Oh, I can think of several sinful events where I have yet to forgive myself, but that has never been a problem for You. As my God, my Father and Mother, my Friend and Companion Along the Way, You always guided, always grieved whenever I lose the path, and always forgive when I did not prove strong enough. Your total acceptance of who I am and Your consistency in remaining by my side through it all has brought me to this place where I begin see my value through Your eyes. My soul and being are totally unique and You crave to have my uniqueness with You always. How could I ever turn away from that kind of love? I am here Lord, Yours forever. Amen."

BE A BETTER PERSON
Reflection: Did I Forget To Say Thank You?

The wife and mother of three and her quietly nodding husband gave this witness to me: Several years ago, her husband had fallen gravely ill and needed an operation. He refused to undergo the procedure for he knew that to do so would result in his death. No one, not doctors or family, could convince him that by not having the operation he would surely die.

So sick he could no longer work, he was released from his job. The family first applied for disability and then welfare. Bills mounted and payments fell behind. The time came when the rent was long overdue and there were not even enough ingredients to make another mulligan stew.

Their three children had become soundless with fear. Daily talk, daily tears, and daily lack all brought home the message that their secure little world was cracking beneath their tiny feet. A public violent, physical jolt is better than the quiet, unobserved quaking of one's own heart.

Mother also felt the fear of loss. She was helpless to change her husband's mind and all prayers uttered up to this point had yet to make a difference. The father of the children would rather destroy the family than die. Who could argue with this?

A stranger did. He came to their door with cash in an envelope and bags of groceries held in his ample arms. Importantly, in his hip pocket was a small copy of the New

Testament. After the children had been fed and put to bed, the stranger encouraged the wife to go take a long, hot soak. He sat down across the kitchen table and looked at the sick, withdrawn, scared husband.

"I heard you were a Christian," said the stranger. "The church I belong to is on the corner of this street and I overheard your neighbors talking about what was happening in this apartment. Are you a Christian?"

"Oh, yes," whispered the tired and depressed husband. "My faith is everything to me. Actually, it is the only thing keeping me from committing suicide."

This was all the stranger needed to hear! He proceeded to take the ailing man on a journey through the New Testament. By the evenings' end this husband and father proclaimed that he now understood the healing power of the Lord and how his fear was not in keeping with His teachings. With newfound courage and conviction, the dying man stated that he would have the life-saving operation.

The operation was a success. The husband/father got well, found another good paying job, bills were paid off and college funds were started for the children.

At the end of hearing about their experiences, I said, "Wow, what a witness story! Come to the Sunday adult class and share your story. It is pure inspiration, and all would benefit from hearing it! As a matter of fact, please consider joining the class. What role models!" I enthusiastically cried out.

"What time is the class?" the husband inquired.

"Eight-thirty every Sunday morning," I eagerly replied.

"Are you kidding?" the wife laughingly stated. "I hardly roll out of bed in time for church! The kids have yet to get to Sunday school. It's our only morning for sleeping in and we're surely not going to give that up!"

Okay, God, You know this situation well. Upon demand, You are to be on hand whenever and wherever You are needed, for however long—but, please, don't expect a return. Once our problem is resolved, we seem to forget to say, "Thank you, God," in thought, word, and deed.

Scriptural Readings by Johnson & McCormick

Mark 1.40-45 "A man suffering from a virulent skin-disease came to him and pleaded on his knees saying, 'If you are willing, you can cleanse me.' Feeling sorry for him, Jesus stretched out his hand, touched him and said to him, 'I am willing. Be cleansed.' And at once the skin-disease left him and he was cleansed. And at once Jesus sternly sent him away and said to him, 'Mind you tell no one anything, but go and show yourself to the priest, and make the offering for your cleansing prescribed by Moses as evidence to them.' The man went away, but then started freely proclaiming and telling the story everywhere, so that Jesus could no longer go openly into any town, but stayed outside in deserted places. Even so, people from all around kept coming to him." New Jerusalem Bible

Luke 17.11-19 "On the way to Jerusalem he [Jesus] entered a village, where he was met by ten lepers who stood at a distance and lifted up their voices and said, 'Jesus, Master, have mercy one us.'

"'Go and show yourselves to the priests,' he said.

"As they went they were cleansed, and one of them, a Samaritan, turned back, praising God with a loud voice; and he fell on his face at Jesus' feet, giving him thanks. 'Were not ten cleansed?' Jesus asked. 'Where are the nine? Was no one found to return and give praise to God except this foreigner? Rise and go your way; your faith has made you well.'" The Reader's Digest Bible

Today's Prayer "Forgive my ignorance, dear Father, in not appreciating the innumerable blessings and gifts You have given to me. Every hour of every day I take so much for granted. One of the greatest gifts I take for granted is that You will always be where I need You to be. The challenge for today and certainly for the rest of my days is to also be where You need me. Together, in partnership; You, my heart and I, Your mouth, and legs. Amen."

BE A BETTER PERSON
Reflection: Words That Really Hurt

"I love you"   "I'm sorry"
          "I want you"   "Forget it"
                    "I like you"   "That's all right"
                              "I forgive you"

How in the world can these great words *hurt?*

When I doubt you are being totally honest.

When you have a history of throwing a past deed back in my face.

Whenever your eyes are not saying what your mouth is.

When your next "hello" is just a little bit cooler.

When, in a joke or joking manner, that "incident' is mentioned.

When you say you thought you meant it at the time you said it, but now:

"I no longer love you."   "I'm not sorry."

"I don't want you anymore."   "Don't forget it."

"I don't like you."   "It's not alright."

"I can't forgive you."

Today I am going to accept at face value what is said to me. I will not look beyond the words. I will not remember the past. Today is new and so am I. And in my heart God and I will make you and our relationship new too—into the Kingdom now.

Please join me.

Scriptural Readings by Johnson & McCormick

Ezekiel 11.19 "I will give them an undivided heart and put a new spirit in them; I will remove from them their heart of stone and give them a heart of flesh." New International Version, The Living Insights Study Bible

2Corinthians 4.16-17 "No wonder we do not lose heart! Though our outward humanity is in decay, yet day by day we are inwardly renewed.

Our troubles are slight and short-lived; and their outcome an eternal glory which outweighs them far." The New English Bible

Revelation 21.1 "Then I saw a new heaven and a new earth, for the first heaven and the first earth had vanished, and there was no longer any sea." The New English Bible

Today's Prayer "Father, I don't want to speak with a 'forked' tongue and I don't want to speak from any 'hidden' agenda. If I cannot sincerely mean 'sorry', 'forgive', 'forget', 'love', then I must not say them. If I do, then I must not get angry, hurt, or disappointed when others insincerely speak those words back to me. I need to accept people for who they are and where they are in their spiritual journey.

I must always remember that Jesus never lied. People could—and have—gone to their death counting on the truthfulness of His words. I want people to feel the same way about the words I speak to them. That I never lie, never exaggerate, never lead them to believe anything other than the truth—even if it is nothing more than my truth. Now that is a reputation worth living into! Help me reach this goal, oh Lord, so that I might glorify God's kingdom here on earth. Amen."

BE A BETTER PERSON
Reflection: Words That Really Heal

"I love you"   "I'm sorry"
          "I want you"   "Forget it"
                    "I like you"   "That's all right"
                              "I forgive you"

I bask in the glow of your acceptance of who I am as a person. I thrive on your goodwill.

Your forgiveness makes me want to do better the next time.

Your apology puts us in the same human pool of imperfection, and I will also excuse myself the next time and the next time and the—.

Your understanding allows me to stop and look at myself. If I do not like either what you saw, what you experienced, then your understanding will help me change. Thanks, friend.

It is easy to love. Jesus calls us to love and since we can readily see each other's humanity, one another's struggles, and since we know that God loves each one of us unconditionally, I too can love. But 'like'? Thank you, dear Lord, for not commanding like. *Like* is hard. Like has many, many variables, yet I can see in your eyes that you truly like me. This is good. I feel good. Thanks, friend.

Today I am going to tell people whichever is appropriate: "I love you." "I'm sorry." "I want you." "Forget it." "I like you." "That's all right." "I forgive you." Because I mean it like you mean it, today the world will be a better place. Thanks, friend.

Today, reach out to your family, friends, coworkers and say the words that bind your relationship with them. Do this and today your world will be a better place.

Scriptural Readings by Johnson & McCormick

John 3.16 "For God so loved the world, that he gave his only begotten Son, that whosoever believeth in him should not perish, but have everlasting life." King James (1611) 1873

1Thessalonians 4.3-12 & 5.12-21 "For this is the Will of God, your sanctification: that you abstain from fornication; that each one of you know how to control your own body in holiness and honor, not with lustful passion, like the Gentiles who do not know God; that no one wrong or exploit a brother or sister in this matter, because the Lord is an avenger in all these things, just as we have already told you beforehand and solemnly warned you. For God did not call us to impurity but in holiness. Therefore who rejects this rejects not human authority but God, who also gives his Holy Spirit to you. Now concerning love of the brothers and sisters, you do not need to have anyone write to you, for you yourselves have been taught by God to love one another; and indeed you do love all the brothers and sisters throughout Macedonia. But we urge you, beloved, to do so more and more, to aspire to live quietly, to mind your own affairs, and to work with your hands, as we directed you, so that you may behave properly toward outsiders and be dependent on no one."

"But we appeal to you, brother and sisters, to respect those who labor among you, and have charge of you in the Lord and admonish you; esteem them very highly in love because of their work. Be at peace among yourselves. And we urge you, beloved, to admonish the idlers, encourage the fait hearted, help the weak, be patient with all of them. See that none of you repays evil for evil, but always seek to do good to one another and to all. Rejoice always, pray without ceasing, give thanks in all circumstances; for this is the Will of God in Christ Jesus for you. Do not quench the Spirit. Do not despise the words of prophets, but test everything; hold fast to what is good; abstain from every form of evil." New Revised Standard Version

Today's Prayer "Thank you, Lord Jesus, for the guidance of Your words and works. In the following of Your examples, I will never be anything other than a person of truth and goodwill. I will want to express love, faithfulness, and obedience, for it is through these acts that I touch the Godhead. Others will come to know You through me. I can think of no greater gift than this to give to You—that I might be the cause of another accepting Your salvation. Just the thought fills my entire being with awe. God is truly great! Amen and Amen."

BE A BETTER PERSON
Reflection: Operating Room Miracle Or The Importance of Getting A Second Opinion

The doctor sliced and gently lifted the breast tissue, scrapping out cells into the Petri dish. He next took a long needle and extracted fluid from an underarm lymph node. Nodding to the nurse to remove the specimens and take them to the waiting pathologist, he leaned back away from the operating table and buried his heart and soul in the Wagner music being piped in. The nurse returned as the Wagnerian grandeur reached a soprano apex that caused the rest of the operating room staff to cringe. But the doctor simply swooned and smiled kindly at a nurse who very much reminded him of his mother.

"Doctor," said the returning nurse. "I had the pathologist check this twice but there is no mistake. No cancer cells exist in either sample. How is this possible?"

The doctor forgot his pleasure. "What," he screamed above the music, "I don't make mistakes like this. He must be wrong."

"No, sir, really he isn't," replied the nurse nervously. Not even the operatic music quelled his bad temper, and she did not want to feel the brunt of it.

"Well, I won't have it. This makes me look bad! Someone turn off the damn music!"

In the abrupt silence, the doctor quickly ran through all the possible scenarios. Ah, he remembered, this patient had seen no necessary reason to get a second opinion, not wanting to take the time. But she did have a prayer group in the waiting room, awaiting news.

"Well," thinks the doctor aloud, "it looks as though their prayers have been answered! As no second opinion can call my initial diagnosis wrong, who can say a miracle hasn't taken place!"

Scriptural Readings by Johnson & McCormick

2Kings 5.11-14 "But Naaman went away angry and said, 'I thought that he would surely come out to me and stand and call on the name of the Lord his God, wave his hand over the spot and cure me of my leprosy. Are not Abana and Pharpar, the rivers of Damascus, better than any of the waters of Israel? Couldn't I wash in them and be cleansed?' So he turned and went off in a rage. Naaman's servants went to him and said, 'My father, if the prophet had told you to do some great thing, would you not have done it? How much more, then, when he tells you, Wash and be cleansed!' So he went down and dipped himself in the Jordan seven times, as the man of God had told him, and his flesh was restored and became clean like that of a young boy." New International Version, The Living Insights Study Bible

Matthew 9.20-22 "Just then a woman who had been subject to bleeding for twelve years came up behind him and touched the edge of his cloak. She said to herself, 'If I only touch his cloak, I will be healed.'

"Jesus turned and saw her. 'Take heart, daughter,' he said, 'your faith has healed you.' And the woman was healed from that moment." New International Version, The Living Insights Study Bible

Today's Prayer "Dear God, why am I so quick to believe what others tell me? I know mistakes are made all the time. We rush through our work, and we pride ourselves on being able to do several things at once, so of course mistakes happen. When it concerns health, I must slow down and insist that all information is correct. A second opinion will be sought. And prayer requests will be asked of everyone, known and unknown. And, if this situation is blessed with a miracle healing as I pray it will be, then all will know of Your work and marvel at Your power. Nothing will be left to chance, for a misdiagnosis only gives excuses and reasons for denying Your existence. Sometimes it is through Your miracles that people come to realize that Your Son and Spirit are actively operating in their lives. Help me, O Lord, be not afraid of any trial placed in my path but teach me to rely on You for, in this reliance, I shall find Your miracle. Amen."

BE A BETTER PERSON
Reflection: The Seduction

My dearest friend had a daughter who was a registered nurse, working in the cystic fibrosis ward at our local children's hospital. Hers was a most demanding job and one I certainly could not do. Watch children die. How does one have the heart and nerves to stand such grief?

For AnnMarie, the answer was by telling stories. AnnMarie told the children marvelous tales about Jesus. What Heaven is like, how gentle and kind God is, how Mother Mary listens to children's prayers, and how a Guardian Angel sits on each bed silently protecting the child from harm. Everyone loved AnnMarie's happy endings.

Cystic fibrosis children make many visits to the hospital. Sometimes their stays are lengthy. AnnMarie soon became a favorite, not only among the children but with their parents. She became the most requested nurse on staff. Each family clamored for her attention, children claimed her friendship, and each dying child's fear was calmed by her soothing touch.

No one knew the real AnnMarie, the young lady whose heart ached for her patients. They only knew the cheerful, smiling nurse who held their hands and told the most awesome stories about life in the Hereafter. Her stories became real, and better than life. They were so wonderful that AnnMarie seduced herself right into death's arms. It was a death where she could join all those children whose hands she had held while they struggled, attempting to take their last gasping breath.

Her suicide came as a terrible shock to those of us who knew and loved her. We never knew the depth of her despair. She never let us in on the fact that the mask she wore had become her great seducer.

How many of us are being seduced by the mask we wear? To what end is our mask leading us?

"WE WEAR THE MASK: We wear the mask that grins and lies,
It hides our cheeks and shades our eyes.
This debt we pay to human guile;
With torn and bleeding hearts we smile,
And mouth with myriad subtleties.
Why should the world be overwise,
In courting all our tears and sighs?
Nay, let them only see us, while
We wear the mask.
We smile,
but,
O great Christ, our cries
To thee from tortured souls arise.
We sing, but oh the clay is vile
Beneath our feet, and long the mile;
But let the world dream otherwise,
We wear the mask!"
Paul Laurence Dunbar (1872-1906)

Scriptural Readings by Johnson & McCormick

Luke 20.46.47 "And in the hearing of all the people he [Jesus] said to his disciples, 'Beware of the scribes, who like to go about in long robes, and love salutations in the marketplaces and the best seats in the synagogues and the places of honor at feasts, who devour widows' houses and for a pretense make long prayers. They will receive the greater condemnation."
The Reader's Digest Bible

Matthew 12.22-37 "Then a demon-possessed man - he was both blind and unable to talk - was brought to Jesus, and Jesus healed him so that he could both speak and see. The crowd was amazed. 'Maybe Jesus is the Messiah!' they exclaimed. But when the Pharisees heard about the miracle they said, He can cast out demons because he is Satan, king of devils.' Jesus knew their thoughts and replied, 'A divided kingdom ends in ruin. A city or home divided against itself cannot stand. And if Satan is casting out Satan, he is fighting himself, and destroying his own kingdom. And if, as you claim, I am casting out demons by invoking the powers of Satan, then what power do your own people use when they case them out? Let them answer your accusation! But if I am casting out demons God has arrived among you. One cannot rob Satan's kingdom without first binding Satan. Only then can his demons be cast out! Anyone who isn't helping me is harming me. Even blasphemy against me or any other sin, can be forgiven - all except one: speaking against the Holy Spirit shall never be forgiven either in this world or in the world to come. A tree is identified by its fruit. A tree from a select variety produces good fruit; poor varieties don't. You brood of snakes! How could evil men like you speak what is good and right? For a man's heart determines his speech. A good man's speech reveals the rich treasures within him. An evil-hearted man is filled with venom, and his speech reveals it. And I tell you this, that you much give account on Judgment Day for every idle word you speak. Your words now reflect your fate then: either you will be justified by them or you will be condemned.'" The Jesus Book

NOTE: Rev. DJ offers two scriptural offerings, each representing masks at its worse, one a person who showed himself before the world a pretender of spirituality and the other who offered a falsified friendship:

Luke 18.10-14 "'Two men went up to the temple to pray, one a Pharisee and the other a tax-collector. The Pharisee stood up and prayed this prayed: 'I thank you, God, that I am not like the rest of mankind - greedy, dishonest, adulterous - or, for that matter, like this tax-collector. I fast twice a week; I pay tithes on all that I get.' But the other kept his distance and would not even raise his eyes to heaven, but beat upon his breast, saying 'God, have mercy on me, sinner that I am.' It was this man, I [Jesus] tell you, and not the other, who went home acquitted of his sins. For everyone who exalts himself will be humbled, and whoever humbles himself will be exalted.'" Revised English Bible

John 6.71 "He [Jesus] was speaking of Judas son of Simon Iscariot, for he, though one of the twelve, was going to betray him." New Revised Standard Version

Hope exists for Jesus goes behind the mask to enlighten our lives as seen in

John 9.5 "While I am in the world I am the light of the world." The New English Bible

Today's Prayer "Father in Heaven, today I hid myself, not once but several times. Somehow, it is all right for You know who I am, but I had yet to find the courage to truly expose myself—warts and all, to other people. I mean, we play so many roles in life: mate, lover, parent, instructor, leader, boss, disciplinarian, and on goes the list. Each different role makes it easier to come across as a little bit more or a little bit less than who I know myself to be. I know that primarily it is fear, fear of appearing different, fear of not being liked or accepted, fear of making a mistake—fear, fear, fear, that holds me back!

Jesus walked among danger every day. He knew that He needed to be about His Father's business and kept His mind focused on the job at hand. We don't see fear in Jesus' work, just obedience. Jesus didn't worry about being liked. He knew Your love and that love gave Him a reality that we, too, can readily offer a response. I know You want this for me also. I am going to try harder to be the authentic me. Your love for me, and Your patience, will enable me to put the masks aside. Just image: maskless! Amen."

BE A BETTER PERSON
Reflection: Need-The Feeding Machine

The anhinga totipalmate's feet slowly paddled in a circle, his keen eyes seeking a ripple among the gently rolling waves. Suddenly he drove into the warm Florida water and just as quickly re-immerged. His beak clenched a fish larger than his head and about as long as his lengthy and flexible neck. An Ahab-and-the-whale struggle began. Foolishly this anhinga allowed hunger to overcome common sense. He fought, dunking the fish over and over, all the time forcing his neck muscles to close his beak tighter and tighter.

The fish fought for life.

The fish won.

For just one split second, the anhinga relaxed his fierce hold to take a deep breath. He probably was gathering strength for the Big Kill.

But the fish's will to live was greater than the anhinga's greed.

That's right. Greed.

Flying away in frustration, the anhinga returned ten minutes later looking the worst for wear. This is a good fishing spot and success comes from retrying. Within seconds, the totipalmate emerged victorious from the waters. This time the fish was just the right size. Swallowed in a flash, the anhinga flew away, his hunger finally satiated.

How many times and in how many ways do we allow our needs to grow out of proportion?

Where does reasonable need end and greed begin?

Scriptural Readings by Johnson & McCormick

2Samuel 11.26-12 10 But when Benaiah went and told Bathsheba that her husband and his friend Uriah had died, she lifted her voice in a loud wail of lamentation. She went into her courtyard and paced continually, weeping and wringing her hands. David watched her from his lofty gardens. He watched for seven days, a proper period for mourning. On the first day of the third week, King David sent Tobias and ten royal maidservants to Uriah's house with crimson garments, a gold necklace, and an onyx brooch carved white on black. They returned to the palace with the pale Bathsheba now robed in exquisite raiment, and she became his wife. Late in the winter, during the latter rains when almond trees bloomed white in the streets of Jerusalem, Bathsheba gave birth to a son. She never named the child. David thought to name him, for the baby was alabaster, fragile, translucent, and his father's heart was moved by the pale beauty and the weakness of the tiny boy. But David was interrupted. A prophet named Nathan requested an audience, saying he could not wait till the child was circumcised. The matter wanted an immediate judgment.

"'Sir," said Nathan, 'two men have a dispute. The one is rich, with many flock and herds. The other is so poor that he had but one little ewe lamb which he brought up with his children. She used to eat from his table, as dear as a daughter to him. Now, a traveler came to the rich man, but he was unwilling to give up any of his own sheep, so he seized the poor man's lamb and slaughtered her and cooked her for his visitor's food.'

"When David heard the nature of the dispute and the injustice done to someone so powerless, he was outraged. 'As the Lord lives,' he said, 'anyone who can do such a thing deserves to die.'

"'Is that,' said Nathan, 'the king's judgment?' David said, 'Surely the rich man must restore to the poor man four times what he took."

"Nathan said," 'How does one restore a life?'

"David looked at the prophet with exasperation." "Even a rich man can't make the dead to live again."

"'Exactly,' Nathan said. He took a stand immediately before the king and said, 'David, you are that rich man. As for the poor man, thus says the Lord: *I delivered you from Saul. I gave you the houses of Judah and of Israel. I gave you wives - and if that were too little, I would add as much more. Why, then, have you despised the word of the Lord? Why have you slain Uriah the Hittite with the weapons of the Ammonites - and then taken his wife to be your wife?'*"
The Book of God

Psalm 17.8-13 "Keep me as the apple of the eye, hide me under the shadow of thy wings. From the wicked that oppress me, from my deadly enemies, who compass me about. They are enclosed in their own fat: with their mouth they speak proudly. They have now compassed us in our steps: they have set their eyes bowling down to the earth; like as a lion that is greedy of his prey, and as it were a young lion lurking in secret places. Arise, 0 Lord, disappoint him, cast him down: deliver my soul from the wicked, which is thy sword." King James Version

Proverbs 1.17-19 "For in vain is the net baited while the bird is looking on; yet they lie in wait - to kill themselves! And set an ambush - for their own lives! Such is the end of all who are greedy for gain; it takes away the life of its possessors." New Revised Standard Version

Isaiah 56.11 "Greedy dogs, never satisfied, such as the shepherds, who understand nothing; they all go their own way, each to the last man after his own interest." New Jerusalem Bible

Luke 12.34 "For where your treasure is, there will your heart be also." Bishops' Bible 1568 (1602)

Today's Prayer "Lord, I can always tell when the Holy Spirit is not within me for, I become greedy. Oh, it's not a bad greed, just a coveting of my neighbor's goods. In these moments, I want more money, a larger car, a bigger house—ah, the 'more', the 'larger', the 'bigger', the mother words to 'greed'. I never like myself after these spells of greed, as I have again walked in the footsteps of unrighteousness. I don't want my life to be about perfecting the art of accumulation.

If I am to collect anything, let it be good deeds.

Help me, my God, to maintain an appreciation for the artisans and architects of this world without needing to acquire their products.

I want to get to that place where I continually enjoy all the fruits of Your labor, oh God. The world You created is a miracle to behold and it doesn't cost a cent to appreciate and enjoy.

The best things in life *are* free and they don't clutter my world with distractions. Help me keep it simple, Lord, so that I might concentrate on You and not on 'Them', those inanimate objects of the world. I would rather live in Your breathing, living Spirit. Amen."

Hundreds of books have been published on the need to "unclutter" our lives, so I am not the only one with the problem of "mine", "I want", "I must have". The first thing needing to go is the "I". Can you do this: Get rid of "I" when it comes to the acquiring of more, larger, bigger?

BE A BETTER PERSON
Reflection: From The Computer Game "Freecell"

Time to take a break. The wordsmith is tired, drained. Experience has taught that a brisk walk does not refresh, it only causes pain in creaking joints, the same joints that will again be sat upon for the next several hours. Experience has also taught that watching a half-hour of TV only enhances brain deadness. Talking on the phone brings my mind back into the world and the focus becomes 'out there' instead of 'in here'. So, what to do? What will be the pause that truly refreshes? Why, playing a computerized game called FreeCell!

It is a card game like solitaire, played with a normal pack of cards. The cards are set out in 8 rows with four rows containing 7 cards and four rows containing 6 cards. The cards lay face up on top of one another so that their color and number can be seen. The object of the game is to put the four aces in the in a number sequence, going from high to low. In the upper left-hand corner, there are four slots where you can put cards 'on hold'. A card might be blocking a good move so it can be 'held' until a play for it comes along. These slots are known as 'free', and they allow you to use their space to move large groups of cards all at once. With the free slots empty, the move is easily made. However, if you have used some of the slots, the move cannot be made. You know this by the flashing sign that says "That move requires moving xcards. You only have enough free space to move x cards."

There is something quite compelling about the game's focus. In the intense concentration that takes place, one forgets time, troubles, duties, questions, and gives oneself over to the pure enjoyment of the challenge. Disappointment occurs when all the "free" slots are filled and there are no more moves to be made. When this happens, the computer flashes a sign saying "Sorry, you lost. There are no more legal moves." If the four suits are successfully built the game ends with a sign reading "Game Over. Congratulations, You Win!"

What I love about this game are the choices. When the game has been won, I am asked, "Do you want to play again?" If I lose, I am asked, "Do you want to play again?" And, if for some reason I want to just quit the game, I am asked, "Are you sure you want to quit this game?" and following each of these questions are two blocks, one saying "Yes" and the other saying "No". I now click the mouse on my choice, my decision.

Having thought about my own reaction to the game and its questions, I have decided that if I could ever get the opportunity to "play God", I would set up life in this manner. Instead of allowing people to plow ahead, making the same mistake over and over, I would give them so many moves. If they use them all up, I will flash a sign before them saying, "Sorry, you lost. There are no more legal moves."

But rather than have them suffer needlessly, I would then ask, "Do you want to play again?" For the person who just wants to quit the game, for whatever reason, I would ask, "Are you sure you want to quit this game?" This would cause the person to stop and think. Maybe even decide to stay in and keep working at whatever challenge being faced. Maybe just by asking this question people would stop running away.

And, best of all, for the job well done, for the spiritual breakthrough, for another steppingstone successfully jumped, I would, in big bold letters announce, "Congratulations, You Win!" And then I would ask, "Do you want to play again?"

Scriptural Readings by Johnson & McCormick

Matthew 1.18-25 "This is how the birth of Jesus Christ came about. His mother Mary was betrothed to Joseph; before their marriage she found she was going to have a child through the Holy Spirit. Being a man of principle, and at the same time wanting to save her from exposure, Joseph made up his mind to have the marriage contract quietly set aside. He had resolved on this, when an angel of the Lord appeared to him in a dream and said, 'Joseph, son of David, do not be afraid to take Mary home with you to be your wife. It is through the Holy Spirit that she has conceived. She will bear a son; and you shall give him the name Jesus, for he will save his people from their sins.' All this happened in order to fulfil what the Lord declared through the prophet: 'A virgin will conceive and bear a son, and he shall be called Emmanuel', a name which means 'God is with us'. When he woke Joseph did as the angel of the Lord had directed him; he took Mary home to be his wife, but had no intercourse with her until her son was born. And he named the child Jesus." Revised English Bible

"Any of those in which Jesus heals, casts out demons, or otherwise 'saves' - so that those receiving a healing might 'play again' - i.e., have a new opportunity at life. Read at the following verse to see the impact of Jesus' healing spirit and its example of humanities desire for the opportunity to 'play again' (Rev. D.J.)

Matthew 4.23-25 "Jesus traveled all through Galilee teaching in the Jewish synagogues, everywhere preaching the Good News about the Kingdom of Heaven. And he healed every kind of sickness and disease. The report of his miracles spread far beyond the borders of Galilee so that sick folk were soon coming to be healed from as far away as Syria. And whatever their illness and pain, or if they were possessed by demons, or were insane, or paralyzed - he healed them all. Enormous crowds followed him wherever he went - people from Galilee, and the Ten Cities, and Jerusalem, and from all over Judea, and even from across the Jordan River." The Jesus Book

Today's Prayer "Dear God, when I look back on my life and see how many doors You opened in order to give me yet another chance, I feel overwhelmed by Your Divine Goodness. You are my Encourager, Supporter, and Giver of Opportunity. Life may take away, strip, or cast aside but You send along the Holy Spirit to protect me and nudge me along. In reading the Holy Bible, Jesus' life and words show me the way to healing and to the opportunity to 'pray again'. Thank You Father, for yet another chance. Amen and amen."

BE A BETTER PERSON
Reflection: Are You Sure You Want To Quit This Game?

Best of all I dearly love the question "Are you sure you want to quit this game?" This question can come at any point in the game and its timing is entirely in MY control. After clicking on the word *quit* and getting the question "Are you sure you want to quit this game" to which I answer *yes*, all cards suddenly disappear. Magically, they reappear in the identical order of the game's beginning. Or the urge may happen in the middle of the game, when many cards are 'home' and it looks like everything is going well until I spot a trap. It may be a workable trap, something that can be gotten around with a lot of maneuvering, or it might be a trap that after a dozen or so moves, dooms 'checkmate'. Why should I bother? Why should I waste time? I'll simply start all over.

Do you see its implication for life? If I could play God for just one day, I would give everyone the opportunity to "quit this game". Just think, the opportunity to take back words that angered or hurt, or the chance to cause a different outcome at a business meeting with different statements, or the possibility of making a relationship work by continually responding to discovered hidden needs. Think of the possibilities! Endless scenarios! They are staggering—and yes, totally unrealistic, for in the end *nothing* would get done. There would be no completed projects; probably not even a finished sentence, for the raw truth is that what pleases me will not please others. If I didn't click *quit*—somebody else would!

Life is too serious to be treated as a game. I need to respect its moments and find meaning in its purpose. Maybe then this is the lesson I can take from the game: When things begin to go wrong, I will find the strength to say, "Stop. This is not what was hoped for" and make the necessary changes. These changes will not be so hard to initiate once I put my sight on God and not on myself.

Scriptural Reading by Johnson & McCormick

"Peter's desire to build booths for Jesus, Moses and Elijah at the Transfiguration versus Jesus' realistic vantage that 'enthronement' is not what His life is all about gives illustration to the fact that our lives are to be lived in and toward a higher purpose." (Rev. DJ)

Mark 9.2-8   "After six days Jesus took Peter, James, and John and led them up a high mountain apart by themselves. And he was transfigured before them, and his clothes became dazzling white, such as no fuller on earth could bleach them. Then Elijah appeared to them along with Moses, and they were conversing with Jesus. Then Peter said to Jesus in reply, 'Rabbi, it is good that we are here! Let us make three tents: one for you, one for Moses, and one for Elijah.' He hardly knew what to say, they were so terrified. Then a cloud came, casting a shadow over them; then from the cloud came a voice, 'This is my beloved Son. Listen to him.' Suddenly, looking around, they no longer saw anyone but Jesus alone with them." New American Bible

John 19.8-16   "Now when Pilate heard this, he was more afraid than ever. He entered his headquarters again and asked Jesus, 'Where are you from?' But Jesus gave him no answer.

Pilate therefore said to him, 'Do you refuse to speak to me? Do you not know that I have power to release you, and power to crucify you?' Jesus answered him, 'You would have no power over me unless it had been given you from above; therefore the one who handed me over to you is guilty of a greater sin.' From then on Pilate tried to release him, but the Jews cried out, "If you release this man, you are no friend of the emperor. Everyone claims to be a king sets himself against the emperor.'

"When Pilate heard these words, he brought Jesus outside and sat on the judge's bench a t a place called The Stone Pavement, or in Hebrew Gabbatha. Now it was the day of Preparation for the Passover, and it was about noon. He said to the Jews, 'Here is your king!' They cried out, 'Away with him! Away with him! Crucify him!' Pilate asked them, 'Shall I crucify your King?' The chief priests answered, We have no king but the emperor.' Then he handed him over to them to be crucified." New Revised Standard Version

Today's Prayer "Father, I sometimes treat life as a game, where there are winners and losers, and events whose outcome I have the power to influence. Sometimes this happens with ease, and every time it does, I am never happy with the outcome. Yet, whenever You were at the helm, I was not disappointed with the results. That is because for You none of life is a game. Teach me, Lord, to be more respectful of what is and more appreciative of what, in Your name, can be. Amen."

BE A BETTER PERSON
Reflection: From Blahs To Ennui

"I am but a shell of my former self" = A statement meaning those elements that feed the spark—one's spirit—are gone, missing. They are the elements of joy, laughter, enthusiasm, curiosity, interest, a sense of purpose, excitement, challenge, hope, need, touch, love, and fulfillment. These are considered essential elements for the health and wellbeing of a balanced life.

When essential elements are missing, the human verges on insanity.

Take away an element or two and you have a simple case of the blahs. Take three or more elements away and one suffers from emotional depression. Lose more and a severe depression develops, requiring anti-depressants. So necessary, so powerful are these elements of touch, feeling and need that their absence can cause chemical imbalances within the brain. The next step in the slide toward Hell's dungeon is a place you never want to go, not ever. There are no short visits, and there are no easy climbs out of this black hold, void of any feeling, any spark. To recreate or resurrect a life glow takes hard, hard work.

Knowing this, one would think we humans would put up a tremendous fight to avoid such misery. At the first sign of the blahs, one would think we would immediately plunge into self-examination to find the missing element and bring it back into our lives. Realizing its importance, one would think we would give the missing element a rebirth and hold on to it for dear life. But we don't. We laugh at the blah and ignore its many warning signs.

It is not until we are in the throes of an ennui attack—meaning a black place of feeling utter weariness or discontent—that we begin to experience a true concern over our wellbeing. Suddenly we realize the deadening boredom and acute lack of interest is not normal. "Oh, my," we so belatedly think, "something must be wrong!" We need to stop being neglectful. We must take whatever steps necessary to cease the downward spiral by immediately examining the cause of the blahs. Warning signs are gifts from God. They exist as godly messages and if we but respect their existence, we can be saved a great deal of grief.

The first step is to realize that the blahs we are experiencing are being caused by a missing essential element. We need to examine our life. Are we being fed *daily* doses of love, touch, interest, curiosity, challenge, excitement, need, hope, a sense of purpose, a feeling of fulfillment, enthusiasm, laughter, and joy? If not, what needs to be done to bring the missing element back into our life? Suffering from the blahs need not cause worry. Rather, it can become a delightful and challenging quest as we begin to rediscover that these elements are gifts from God, our beloved Creator of all that is and of all that will be. God made these gifts essential for our wellbeing so that we could live a wholesome life. The blahs are just a little nudge from God that says, "Hey, wake up! There's a piece missing in your quest for 'wholeness' - or is that 'holiness'!"

Scriptural Readings by Johnson & McCormick

The difficulty of restoring faithfulness is complicated by the snowball effect: Bad decision lead to other bad decisions; thus, the importance of seeking God in everyday life. P. M.

Luke 22.31-34 "Simon, Simon, behold, Satan demanded to have you, that he might sift you like wheat, but I have prayed for you that your faith may not fail; and when you have turned again, strengthen your brethren."

"'Lord,' said Peter, 'I am ready to go with you to prison and to death.'"

"'I tell you, Peter,' Jesus said, 'the cock will not crow this day, until you three times deny that you know me.'"

Luke 22.54-62 "Then they seized him (Jesus) and led him away to the high priest's house. At a distance, Peter followed, and in the courtyard he sat down among the guards and servants at the fire. Then a main, gazing at him, said, 'This man also was with him'. Peter said, 'Woman, I do not know him.' A little later some one else saw him and said, 'You also are one of them.'"

"'Man, I am not,' said Peter. After an interval of about an hour still another insisted, 'Certainly this man also was with him; for he is a Galilean.'"

"'Man,' said Peter, 'I do not know what you are saying.' And immediately, while he was still speaking, the cock crowed. And the Lord turned and looked at Peter, and Peter remembered how he had said to him, "Before the cock crows today, you will deny me three times.' And he went out and wept bitterly."
The Reader's Digest Bible

John 15.1-8 "'I am the real vine,' and my Father is the gardener. Every barren branch of mine he cuts away; and every fruiting branch he cleans, to make it more fruitful still. You have already been cleansed by the word that I spoke to you. Dwell in me, as I in you. No branch can bear fruit by itself, but only if it remains united with the vine; no more can you bear fruit, unless you remain united with me."

"'I am the vine,' and you the branches. He who dwells in me, as I dwell in him, bears much fruit; for apart from me you can do nothing. He who does not dwell in me is thrown away like a withered branch. The withered branches are heaped together, thrown on the fire, and burnt."

"'If you dwell in me, and my words dwell in you, ask what you will, and you shall have it. This is my Father's glory, that you may bear fruit in plenty and so be my disciples.'" The New English Bible

1Corinthians 13.1-2 "If I speak in human and angelic tongues, but do not have love, I am a resounding gong or a clashing cymbal. And if I have the gift of prophecy and comprehend all mysteries and all knowledge; if I have all faith so as to move mountains, but do not have love, I am nothing." New American Bible

Today's Prayer "Dear God, too many times my eyes have not seen, my ears have not heard, my heart has not felt, my body has not responded to, my mind has not comprehended, and my soul has not sung to the wonders of life. You have given it wholly to me *plus* the daily reminders of just how important it all is. Lord and Spirit, help me be aware and vigilant and discount nothing. Amen."

Where are you right now? Are you within yourself, or are you with God, loving, forgiving, Father, who craves nothing more than to be a part of your life? Is it not wonderful to think of that? God wanting to be with you, in your mind, in your heart, hearing, suggesting, being your personal helpmate through living your daily life?

Open up. Let Him in. You will never, ever be sorry. The Holy Spirit will wrap you in protection, our Healing Lord will salve your hurts, while Father leads the way.

BE A BETTER PERSON
Reflection: Taking Care Of Business

"For want of a nail the shoe was lost,
for want of a shoe the horse was lost
for want of a horse the rider was lost,
for want of a rider the battle was lost,
for want of a battle the kingdom was lost,
and all for the want of a horseshoe nail."

People coming into my room see a small basket hanging on the wall, about halfway up. They think it is for decorative purposes and in need of silk flowers. I do nothing to improve their misinterpretation of the basket's use. To date, only one person has stuck fingers inside and discovered the tiny scraps of paper. I almost died. Seeing the expression on my face, she quietly put them back in and never asked a question. A real friend.

Those papers are a collection of my sins, mistakes, afterthoughts, misdeeds, misdoings, real concerns, and downright ugliness. I want them there, hanging on the wall in mid-space, as a constant reminder of what happens whenever I neglect the obvious, whenever I forget, or ignore the righteousness of order.

There really is a proper way to do things, a right way to live life. I, the bull in the China shop, want everything completed as of yesterday. This might mean some push and shove, or it might mean jumping over, or talking over, or just ignore.

It means not taking the time to eat when hungry, and then taking the hunger out on the nearest person. It means not sending that get well card or birthday wish because a deadline looms, and I'll avoid the hurt-in-eyes look when next we meet. It means being short-tempered, because I am tired because I didn't get enough sleep, because I had to complete this important something that will be meaningless in the tomorrows of hurt feelings.

First things first and the Kingdom will be saved.

Scriptural Readings by Johnson & McCormick

Exodus 20.1-14 "God spoke all these words, saying: I am YHWH your God, who brought you out from the land of Egypt, from a house of serfs. You are not to have any other gods before my presence. You are not to make yourself a carved image or any figure that is in the heavens above, that is on the earth beneath, that is in the waters beneath the earth; you are not to bow down to them, you are not to serve them, for I, YHWH your God, am a jealous God, calling-to-account the iniquity of the fathers upon the sons, to the third and the fourth (generation) of those that hate me, but showing loyalty to the thousandth of those that love me, of those that keep my commandment."

"You are not to take up the name of YHWH your God for emptiness, for YHWH will not clear him that takes up his name for emptiness."

"Remember the Sabbath day, to hallow it. For six days, you are to serve, and are to make all your work, but the seventh day is Sabbath for YHWH your God: you are not to make any kind of work, (not) you, nor your son, nor your daughter, (not) your servant, nor your maid, nor your beast, nor your sojourney that is within your gates.

For in six days YHWH made the heavens and the earth, the sea and all that is in it, and he rested on the seventh day; therefore YHWH gave the Sabbath day his blessing, and he hallowed it."

"Honor your father and your mother, in order that your days may be prolonged on the soil that YHWH your God is giving you. You are not to murder. You are not to adulter. You are not to steal. You are not to testify against your fellow as a false witness. You are not to desire the house of your neighbor, you are not to desire the wife of your neighbor, or his servant, or his maid, or his ox, or his donkey, or anything that is your neighbor's." The Five Books of Moses

Luke 10.38 "As they continued their journey, he [Jesus] entered a village where a woman whose name was Martha welcomed him. She had a sister named Mary (who) sat beside the Lord at his feet listening to him speak. Martha, burdened with much serving, came to him and said, 'Lord, do you not care that my sister has left me by myself to do the serving? Tell her to help me.' The Lord said to her in reply, 'Martha, Martha, you are anxious and worried about many things. There is need of only one thing. Mary has chosen the better part, and it will not be taken from her." New American Bible

Today's Prayer "Dear God in Heaven, out of void and chaos You used order to create this marvelous world of ours. You gave instructions on how we are to be and act within this order. My problems begin whenever I try to take a shortcut or ignore the order placed before me. You made it all so simple: God first, then me. Family next. People, then the world and its environment. It is through the study of Your Word that I grow in understanding of my place and Your Divine need of me."

That first line in the ancient poem needs to read "For want of You, I was lost. Amen."

Is your life in right order? You want to make changes?

Remember, small steps first. This is where your success lies in getting your life in the right order.

BE A BETTER PERSON
Reflection: A Path To Self-Forgiveness

Go with me on a journey. Be in a quiet place where there are no distractions. Settle yourself down and be comfortable. Hold this page in front of your eyes and let its words draw pictures in your mind.

A country path stretches out in front of you. The day is absolutely beautiful. It is the kind of day that makes you truly thankful you are alive. How you are looking forward to walking down the path that is covered overhead with huge branches! Feel this in your heart. Feel the gentle breeze cooling your skin warmed by the sun. Chirping birds call to you and fluffy-tailed squirrels are scampering up and down the massive tree trunks. A variety of colorful flowers line the pathway. You take a deep breath. Listen! There is a family of white-tailed rabbits frolicking among the flowers. You smile and pause a moment to relish your anticipation to begin your journey among God's great creation. Your eyes behold its beauty.

Ah, wait, stop. Before you take a step, think first about a recent sin, a wrongdoing that causes your heart to hurt. Hold the thought in your mind. Look down. See the several different size lumps of dirt lying before your feet? Choose the size lump of dirt that corresponds with the size of your sin. Pick it up and feel its weight in your hand. Now transfer your sin into the lump of dirt. What happened to the color of the dirt? Feel the lump get heavier. For a big sin it is going to be very heavy indeed.

Now begin to walk down the path. Look at all the beauty around you. You desire to be a part of it, but you cannot because of this dirty, heavy lump of sin you are carrying. How are you going to get rid of it so that you can freely join in with the beauty and freedom which surrounds you?

Meditate on the power of God. Think about what life—and living fully in it, means to you. Mix your meaning of living life with the power of God. Mix the two together, round and round. Watch the mixture begin a spiral upwards. As it appears just above eye level, take your sin-filled clump of dirt, and throw it, as hard as you can, into the whirlpool that continues to spin upward. What is happening to your sin in the middle of your desire for living life and God's power?

Watch now. Keep your eyes on the whirling, the turmoil. Is there sound? What do you hear?

Look. Momentarily lost sight of the sin was lost, but there it is now, coming back to earth. Is it traveling fast, too fast to stop, or is it falling slowly downward? Oh, look, the whirling mass has touched the ground. Well, will you look at that!

What now do you see?

Scriptural Readings by Johnson & McCormick

Matthew 11.28-30 "'Come to me,' all whose work is hard, whose load is heavy; and I will give you relief. Bend your necks to my yoke, and learn from me, for I am gentle and humble-hearted; and your souls will find relief. For my yoke is good to bear, my load is light." The New English Bible

James 3.17 "But the wisdom from above is in the first place pure; and then peace-loving, considerate, and open-minded; it is straightforward and sincere, rich in compassion and in deeds of kindness that are its fruit." Revised English Bible

Today's Prayer "I have taken this journey many times, dear Lord, always seeking forgiveness. Paul said it best when he cried aloud to You saying that he does those things he ought not to do and does not do those things that he ought to do. I totally identify with this sentiment. Words fly out of my mouth that ought never to have been thought, much less spoken. Actions and deeds have been committed that cause shame and for which I can never apologize enough."

I want to say "the Devil made me do it" but the only *devil* around is the one residing in a corner of my heart and claiming space in a piece of my mind. Only two realities offer freedom is Your forgiveness of my sins. Please, guide me upon the path of self-forgiveness. Help me realize that I need to forgive myself, for, with my "forgive me, Father" You wiped my slate clean. But I have not forgiven myself.

Forgiveness needs to be a join act, a Divine Action joining Heaven and Earth. Your forgiveness—my self-forgiveness. With Your help I shall be able to live free and in Your glory. Amen."

It is true that God loves us more than we love ourselves. This is why His forgiveness is absolute and incident. God offers, instantaneously, an opportunity for us to move forward. The stumbling block is us. What is it going to take for you to forgive yourself? Answer this question. Now, move forward in action. Talk to who you need to, act to repair. You can do this. You can even tell yourself, "I'm sorry."

BE A BETTER PERSON
Reflection: I Never Thought This Would Happen To Me

a victim of a crime - divorced - downsized - have an affair - face financial ruin - hate someone enough to actually want to cause him/her harm - be a single parent - arrested - disabling accident - outlive my child - lose contact with a family member - forced to lie to save someone or something - be a parent of a criminal - contract a sexually transmitted disease - see a friend die - take prescription drugs - face a lawsuit - have heart problems - have a mentally or physically defected child - fall in love with the wrong person - consider suicide - end up caretaker of your mate - have an addiction problem - be fired for sexual harassment - have the knowledge of facing death in the near future - grow old - begin to doubt the existence of God - lose my faith.

Why not? Why do we feel that none of the above should ever happen to us? We accept the fact that in the process of living we will laugh less and yes, maybe even become somewhat cynical. We know we will, from time to time, feel loneliness, alone, fear, sorrow, anger, empathy, and all other emotions, but have bad things happen to us? NO. That is not part of the plan.

Again, why not?

Because bad things are not supposed to happen to good people.

But they do. And that makes LIFE exceedingly unfair. If a good deed is to be rewarded then, surely, a good life is also to be rewarded. If this is not so, if justice and mercy are just allusions and life is really a matter of DNA, chance, and luck, then why bother? If much of life is a matter of the right place at the right time, then why should we work so hard?

Amid these questions of living through a particularly hellish experience, I ask myself, "Is this indeed all there is?" If existence and life's many struggles are just about the here and now, then what is the point? Why spend a lifetime fighting for improvement, self and otherwise? Does there not have to be more of a point to life than just death at its end? I breathe and then I don't? I awake each day until it never happens again? I heal and then I rot? What kind of a joke is this?

A Holy Bible reading person knows that God's people since Creation have argued over the meaning of life. This argument is not rhetorical for questions, frustrations, and anger at God over life's many disappointments are all part of any individual's spiritual journey. Heartfelt pain or hatred experienced eventually brings understanding and spiritual growth. Sometimes, but not often, an understanding can occur in the middle of a turmoil. Mostly though, time is needed for healing to take place.

As a child of thirteen, on Christmas Eve, I was raped. Christmas immediately took on a different connotation than what God ever intended. Time was needed. I was in my twenties before finally understanding that God was not to blame. Mankind ultimately pays for crimes and misdeeds performed—maybe not legally, but God's justice is done. This is true with willful pollution, needless slaughter, crimes against humanity, hunger, homelessness, and acts of violence.

This coming-to-grips with life's pain versus Free Will issues led to an understanding about time, God, soul, and eternity. I had a choice, just like you do. I could have spent my years carrying around hatred, fear, guilt, and disliking every Christmas and every man for the rest of my life, or I could hand it all over to our Lord and get on with the good things about life and living. I have chosen to live.

Will you join me by laying down your pain and getting on with living a good life?

Scriptural Readings by Johnson & McCormick

Luke 23.34a "Jesus said, 'Father, forgive them; they do not know what they are doing." The New English Bible

Jude 1.17-21 "But, beloved, remember ye the words which were spoken before of the apostles of our Lord Jesus Christ; how that they told you there should be mockers in the last time, who should walk after their own ungodly lusts. These be they who separate themselves, sensual, having not the Spirit. But ye, beloved, building up yourselves on your most holy faith, praying in the Holy Ghost, keep yourselves in the love of God, looking for the mercy of our Lord Jesus Christ unto eternal life." King James Bible (1611) 1873

Today's Prayer "God, I have blamed You for human wrongdoing. I have railed out against You with fury. "Why did YOU allow this to happen?" has been my battle cry more than once. In my heart, I know that You forgave my ignorance in placing blame at Your footstool. You are not and never have been at fault. My family and friends, strangers and enemies are the ones who harm and cause hurt. And, yes, me too, getting so wrapped up in the hour of malevolence that the only thought is to strike back.

And how many times have I felt helpless to do anything, not able to cause another the kind of pain I have felt! How angry I would get that they would not feel my sting. And for what? So that I would end up more like them!"

Thank You, sweet Jesus, for protecting me against myself! Once the turmoil passed, I could again feel Your presence and I could tum to You for protection and healing. You have always helped right the wrongs of this earth. On You I can depend. With You I can find a way through life's pain, horror, disappointments, frustrations and rediscover life's healing, joy, awards, and triumphs. With You, all things are possible. Thank God. Amen."

BE A BETTER PERSON
Reflection: A Path To Other-Forgiveness

You will not be too surprised to learn that the path to forgiveness for other people who have harmed you follows along the same steps as self-forgiveness. There is one major difference though—the object you pick up and put into the palm of your hand is going to be much heavier. It is a human quirk that the self-sin we carry is never quite as heavy, quite as dark, hurtful, or evil, as the sin another committed against us!

This time let's go out into the desert. What better place, but under the dark sky scattered with tiny stars to forgive a hateful deed committed against our personhood! Picture yourself standing still in the middle of a desert. I believe that God created the desert filled with distinctive plants and animals to teach us that, even in harsh environments, we can overcome. Visualize how off to one side is the purplish outline of a mountain whose thin twin peak appears to touch the nearest twinkling star. Off to the other side are ground shadows, outlining various sized boulders and cacti. Take a deep breath. Take in the faint smells of the cacti blooms—so delicate.

Listen now. Let your ears begin to pick up the sounds of creatures crawling. A Fennec fox plays with a scampering kangaroo rat while a deathstalker scorpion seeks a rock's safety. Visualize life among these creatures of God. Feel their pace. Sense their lack of awareness and quiet in the still night air.

A harmless snake slitter across nearby rock while reptiles flee from his sight. All seek the comfort of night. Reach out your arms and feel the space, free space, and wide-open space all around you. Turn around. Turn around.

Stop. Now ask this: would you not like your inner life to be filled with this lightness, this amount of free and open space? Here in the desert God speaks in a whisper. It is here in the desert that angels fed and cared for our Lord. They wait patiently now to feed and care for you.

Sit down. Make yourself comfortable on the desert floor. Feel warmth radiating from the sun's daylong heating. Its heat travels through your skin and sends warmth deep into your bones. Comfortable? Good. Now hold out a hand. Watch an angel come and drop onto your palm a sin another person perpetrated against you. Look at the sin. Which one is it? No, no, not the second or third one you thought of! The very first sin that popped into your mind is the one you are to work on!

Look down into your hand. You no longer see that sin but instead, a leaf from one of the cacti. How long are its thorns? Ah, observe how the thorns are as long as the resentments and anger, disappointments and hatred toward that person are. Now gently close your hand over the thorn cactus leaf. Don't be afraid. The pain will not be more—or less—than the hurt you have already been carrying around within you. In the process of closing your hand over this pain you begin to realize that your emotions are nothing compared to the craving in your heart to possess the freedom of the desert spirit. Now look down at your tightly closed hand with your knuckles so purple and your fingers so white.

On each of your four knuckles sits an angel of our Lord. The first angel sitting on your pinky represents disappointment, the next finger resentment, the next anger, and the finger next to your thumb represents hatred. These angels are waiting for you to release those emotions. You do not have to be told that these emotions are harming your spirit, your life. Do you not deserve better than this?

Let it go. Let it go so that you might live in freedom. Each angel will help you release a finger from your tightly clinched fist. Say a prayer and ask God to guide you. Concentrate on the harm caused by holding on to hurt and sorrow. Once you have worked through the process you begin to rejoice at releasing these feelings and watching them dissolve into nothingness. Look at what is happening to your thumb. Each time a finger is released, the angel leaves it and flies over to your thumb. When you have completely let go of the disappointment, let go of the resentment, let go of the anger, let go of the hatred, you will find that all four angels are now sitting on your thumb, the finger representing forgiveness.

We will now give to this person who caused so much pain and hurt the same kind of total unconditional forgiveness that God gives continually to each one of us. Feel the sense of freedom bestowed upon you upon this the final act. What blest! Rather than any pain in your hand, you become aware of the space and quiet and movement of life in the desert, inside you.

If ever the remembrance of that incident rears its ugly head, immediately wrap your four fingers around your thumb and recall the forgiveness you gave. Do not let the past influence your present. Remember this important lesson: God also totally forgets our sin. Forgetting is a big part of what forgiveness is all about. You and I, we are called to do the same with one another and self.

Scriptural Readings by Johnson & McCormick

Mark 11.24.25 "Listen to me! You can pray for _anything_ and _if you believe, you have it,_ it's yours! But when you are praying, first forgive anyone you are holding a grudge against so that your Father in heaven will forgive you your sins too." The Jesus Book

"I really see non-forgiveness as the thief who comes in the night to steal all that we have, which is why I like the following verse." (P. M.)

John 10.10 "The thiefs purpose is to steal, kill and destroy. My purpose is to give life in all its fullness." The Jesus Book

Today's Prayer   "'Our Father in heaven, hallowed be Your Name, Your kingdom come, Your will be done, on earth as in heaven. Give us today our daily bread. Forgive us our sins AS we forgive those who sin against us.' I repeat this prayer often, dear Lord, sometimes trying not to pay attention to the 'AS' for it is hard. Maybe it is too soon, maybe I am still hurting too much, and maybe I can't see my way through the tangled betrayal. My Lord and God, I am not as You. I cannot forgive so readily, even though I know it is in my best interest to do so. I need Your help, Your guidance through the maze of confusion, fury, and hatred. Touch my heart, dear Lord. I know there is a better way and I want; nay, need to claim it for my own. Place the key of forgiveness in my hand, 0 God, so that the doors to mind and emotion may breath in the Holy Spirit. With Your help, I shall be free. Free to live and love and laugh with a child's joy again. Amen."

Freedom to live free of sin! Is this even possible? Well, I have to say "no" where I am concerned for my faults and flaws are many. But I surround myself with people who, even though they, too, have faults and flaws, are still mentors and exemplars of who I wish to be.

Do you have such people in your life? Look around. Sometimes you can find them in the most unlikely places. Ask our Good Lord to guide you in this journey.

BE A BETTER PERSON
Reflection: My Cat Has Gray Hairs

How dare she! It is one thing for me to look into the mirror and see my own wrinkles and sagging chin line and quite another to look at the cat and see her beautiful deep cocoa brown fur spotted with gray hairs!

How is it that I can readily accept my own aging process but go nuts over the fact that this cat, this nothing but an animal, is also aging?

This is easily answered, for there is nothing deep or mysterious about the question. I do not want to see gray hairs on Miss Cocoa because it forces me to consider a time when she will no longer be here with me.

Dumb animal. I would miss her. Oh, not the cat hairs on my pillow, or her smelly litter box. But her companionship, and the way she never criticizes, not even when I run out of her favorite cat food. I would miss the sound of her purr, and the healing way she remains by my side when sad, troubled, or ailing.

I would miss her because Miss Cocoa is the kind of friend I wish I could find in the human world. Someone to listen upon demand. Someone who would come running when called. Someone who would rather sing than talk. Someone to play with or pray with. Someone with whom to listen to a reading or sit quietly by the roaring fire with equal contentment. Someone to look at me with the eyes of love which never sees the sagging chin line and deepening wrinkles.

Well, I certainly stand convicted in front of these words. How can I ask for someone to be this kind of friend to me when I am not this kind of friend of anyone? I see now where this cat's life has more value than just meeting my needs. Miss Cocoa is teaching me how to meet the needs of others.

Scriptural Readings by Johnson & McCormick

Ruth 1.1-18 "Long ago there was a famine so severe in Israel that Elimelech of Bethlehem took his wife and his two sons to Moab, to survive there until rain returned to Judah. Soon after their journey Elimelech died, and his wife Naomi was left to raise her sons alone. In time each man married a Moabite wife, one whose name was Orpah, one whose name was Ruth. But then her sons died, too, and the woman was bereft altogether. In sorrow she decided to return to her own people.

"Naomi said to her daughters-in-law, 'Go back to your mothers' houses, and may the Lord deal as kindly with you as you have dealt with the dead and with me.' She kissed them, and they began to weep. 'We will go with you to your people, they said. Naomi said, 'Do I have more sons in my womb? Daughters, I am too old to marry, but you should not refrain from marrying again.'

"So Orpah kissed Naomi and departed. But Ruth clung to her. 'Entreat me not to leave you or to return from following you,' Ruth said. 'For where you go I will go, and where you lodge I will lodge. Your people shall be my people, and your God my God. Where you die I will die, and there will I be buried.' Naomi saw that Ruth was determined. She said no more.'"
The Book of God

Matthew 2.13b-15a "suddenly the angel of the Lord appeared to Joseph in a dream and said, 'Get up, take the child and his mother with you, and escape into Egypt, and stay there until I tell you, because Herod intends to search for the child and do away with him' So Joseph got up and, taking the child and his mother with him, left that night for Egypt. Where he stayed until Herod was dead." New Jerusalem Bible

Today's Prayer "Father, life is but a chain of events and within each chain, one can find examples of Your Divinity. Joseph knew love and protection from Your angel. Naomi knew love and loyalty from Ruth, and on it goes, through each story-chain in the Holy Bible and from each story-chain in our own lives. The great lesson is that You talk with us within each chain, whether it be by the whispers of an angel, or a friend making a sacrifice for us, or through the devotion of a household pet. If I but look and listen, Your messages can be heard in the everyday avenues of life. Thank you, my Lord and Christ, for loving enough to send Your message. As the Spirit stands before me, I hear Your words. Amen."

Who speaks to you with the words of love, protection, loyalty, and wisdom? Probably no one person for that is a lot to put on anyone's plate. The more people we invite into our lives, fulfilling one or more of these gifts, the better off we are. Life is fuller, the road easier.

Remember, what is given to you needs to be returned to others.

BE A BETTER PERSON
Reflection: The Self-Made Victim

I woke up this morning and said to myself, "Today is not going to be a good day!"

I looked at the luncheon menu and said to myself, "There is not one single good food item on this list!"

I said the meeting was going to be a waste of time - and guess what!

I knew beforehand that the party was going to be a bore - the movie dull – the book stupid - the conversation pointless; and guess what!

I don't play the game of kissing up for a raise or promotion – and guess what?

As soon as s/he opened her/his mouth, I knew there was going to be a problem.

I thought s/he would fail to understand - and I was right!

I am afraid this is going to turn out bad.

And, of course, I let these expectations—by thought, word, and deed—be known. I allow you to view my 'Demon Apprehension' and tell you of fears or that I expect to be wronged, misunderstood, disappointed, left frustrated or not knowing what to do. And guess what?

It really is bad enough that I make my own self into a victim by prophesying failure and then living into them. But when I lay myself out like this, do you also have to live *down* to my expectations? Must you buy into my fears and make them real? Must you join arms with the 'Demon Apprehension' who resides in my mind? For without you living down to my expectations and without you taking advantage of my situation and words, I could not have successfully turned myself into a victim. But, then again, isn't this the thought-path so often used to become a victim? While I have been bent on momentary self-destruction, have I brought you into my life simply because you easily fit into the pattern of other-destruction?

What would life be like if I refused to be so self-abused? How will life change if I stop placing my fears and apprehensions in front of people, and then act surprised as they take advantage of those fears and apprehensions? What would happen if I stopped putting myself out there, like some weak or sacrificial creature, just asking *for it*—to be so abused—even from my own inner self?

Scriptural Readings by Johnson & McCormick

Exodus 16.1-20 "They moved on from Elim, and they came, the entire community of the Children of Israel, to the Wilderness of Syn, which is between Elim and Sinai, on the fifteenth day after the second New-Moon after their going out from the land of Egypt. And they grumbled, the entire community of the Children of Israel, against Moshe and against Aharon in the wilderness. The Children of Israel said to them: Would that we had died by the hand of YHWH in the land of Egypt, when we sat by the flesh pots, when we ate bread till (we were) satisfied!

For you have brought us into this wilderness to bring death to this whole assembly by starvation! YHWH said to Moshe: Here, I will make rain down upon you bread from the heavens, the people shall go out and glean, each day's amount in its day, in order that I may test them, whether they will walk according to my Instruction or not. But it shall be on the sixth day: when they prepare what they have brought in, it shall be a double portion compared to what they glean day after day.

"Moshe and Aharon said to all the Children of Israel: At sunset you will know that it is YHWH who brought you out of the land of Egypt; at daybreak you will see the Glory of YHWH; when he hearkens to your grumblings against YHWY - what are we, that you grumble against us? Moshe said: Since YHWH gives you flesh to eat at sunset, and at daybreak, bread to satisfy (yourselves) since YHWH hearkens to your grumblings which you grumble against him - what are we: not against us are your grumblings, but against YHWH!

"Moshe said to Aharon: Say to the entire community of the Children of Israel: Come-near, in the presence of YHWH, for he has hearkened to your grumblings!

"Now it was, when Aharon spoke to the entire community of the Children of Israel, they faced the wilderness and here: the Glory of YHWH could be seen in the cloud. YHWH spoke to Moshe, saying: I have hearkened to the grumblings of the Children of Israel - speak to them, and say: Between the setting-times you shall eat flesh, and at daybreak you shall be satisfied with bread, and you shall know that I am YHWH your God.

"Now it was at sunset a horde-of-quail came up and covered the camp. And at daybreak there was a layer of dew around the camp; and when the layer of dew went up, here, upon the surface of the wilderness, something fine, scaly, fine as hoar-frost upon the land.

When the Children of Israel was it they said each-man to his brother: *Mahn hu I* what is it? For they did not know what it was.

"Moshe said to them: It is the bread that YHWH has given you for eating. This is the word that YHWH has commanded: Glean from it, each-man according to what he can eat, an *omer* per capita, according to the number of your persons, each-man, for those in his test, you are to take.

"The Children of Israel did thus, they, gleaned, the-one-more and the-one less, but when they measured by the *omer,* no surplus had the-one-more, and the-one-less had no shortage; each-man had gleaned according to what he could eat.

"Moshe said to them: No man shall leave any of it until morning. But they did not hearken to Moshe, and (several) men let some of it until morning; it became wormy with maggots and reeked. And Moshe became furious with them." The Five Books of Moses

Matthew 7.6-11 "'Do not give dogs what is holy; do not throw your pearls to the pigs: they will only trample on them and turn and tear you to pieces.

"'Ask, and you will receive; seek, and you will find; knock, and the door will be opened to you. For everyone who asks receives, those who seek find, and to those who knock, the door will be opened.

"'Would any of you offer his son a stone when he asks for bread, or a snake when he asks for a fish? If you, bad as you are, know how to give good things to your children, how much more will your heavenly Father give good things to those who ask him!" Revised English Bible

Luke 5.29.32 "Then Levi gave a great banquet for him [Jesus] in his house, and a large crowd of tax collectors and others were at table with them. The Pharisees and their scribes complained to his disciples, saying, 'Why do you eat and drink with tax collectors and sinners?' Jesus said to them in reply, 'Those who are healthy do not need a physician, but the sick do. I have not come to call the righteous to repentance but sinners.'"
New American Bible

Today's Prayer   "My Father, do you know that I know I really don't have to make myself into a victim, serving my own self destructive needs? Yes, of course. You are The One who placed the knowledge in my mind and heart to being with. You are saying that it is past time to put aside this 'victim game'. Thanks to this knowledge, I am now too aware of what is transpiring at the times it is taking place. You gladly show how the irrational fears make me into a victim and You point out how my temper causes me to be an easy victim. Whenever wrong occurs and I don't speak up or speak out, I, ultimately, become a victim of situations or of other people. You have shown me, Father, how I set people, events, and myself up to lose. And You have stated that this is not the way I am to live my life. God, You give this knowledge as motivation to change because You know I don't want to shrink from who You are calling me to be, who I am struggling to grow into, according to Your Divine Will. It is Your will that the victim game stops now.

"Come, Lord Jesus. Infuse in me the Courage of Refusal, that marvelous, wonderful ingredient found within Free Will. No longer will the essence of me be a plaything at the disposal of others or self. Without self-victimization, I shall indeed be able to stand in Your Footsteps and, with the help of the Holy Spirit, soon be able to walk Your way! Like the Children of Israel, I, too, shall learn the lessons of self-care and courage. Amen."

It takes knowledge of self to identify what actions are self-defeating. Identify these, make a list, put them in order from "small" to "harder". Then, get to work. No one can do this but you.

BE A BETTER PERSON
Reflection: Living Within Miracles

At church there is a personable gentleman who was reared in the Jewish faith. In his youth, he studied hard, learned Hebrew, and can euphonically recite its many prayers. At an early age God touched Harry's life, and he responded to God's call. At a later age, Jesus touched Harry's life and again, he responded to the Call.

For me, Harry is a living example of what it was like after the time that Jesus walked this earth. During Jesus' ministry and after His death and resurrection, those in the Jewish communities answered the call of our Lord. Immediately after becoming a Christian, they had to separate themselves from family and friends. They were no longer able to worship in the synagogues, and they were not accepted in Jewish social circles. Suddenly, all that was familiar and easy, and friendly changed. Their lives had to focus totally on Jesus and become acclimated into the New Life. That was then. And today, two thousand years later, this cycle continues. Harry had to leave his old life behind, including family and friends. His Christian family helped him and, by his belief, worship, and presence in our midst, Harry brings the Gospels alive, so much so that he is truly a walking New Testament.

This man is a "Sunday miracle" who brings a sharp awareness of how we experience other miracles throughout the week.

My husband arrives safely home from work after driving on the Interstate and across bridges during rush hour traffic. I also arrive home in the dark after a church vestry meeting, again saved from harm while driving on the dreaded Route 19 which daily creates its roadkill. After all other means failed, an ambulance driver laid hands over the infant's heart and prayed. The baby began to breathe again, her heart beating. A small dog barked and barked until his sleeping family finally awoke to run from the blazing fire. A tornado ravaged the town and destroyed much but not one life was lost while each person tells again and again of how by happenstance they happened to be there or not be there or suddenly safely came in the form of—.

God continues to mightily work in our daily lives.

Scriptural Readings by Johnson & McCormick

2Corinthians 9.10-12 "He who supplies seed to the sower and bread for food will supply and multiply your seed for sowing and increase the harvest of your righteousness. You will be enriched in every way for your great generosity, which will produce thanksgiving to God through us; for the rendering of this ministry not only supplies the needs of the saints but also overflows with many thanksgivings to God." New Revised Standard Version

Luke 8.40-42.49-558 "When Jesus returned, the crowd welcomed him, for they were all waiting for him. And a man named Jairus, an official of the synagogue, came forward. He fell at the feet of Jesus and begged him to come to his house, because he had an only daughter, about twelve years old, and she was dying. As he went, the crowds almost crushed him...

While he was still speaking, someone from the synagogue official's house arrived and said, 'Your daughter is dead; do not trouble the teacher any longer.' On hearing this, Jesus answered him, 'Do not be afraid; just have faith and she will be saved.' When he arrived at the house he allowed no one to enter with him except Peter and John and James, and the child's father and mother. All were weeping and mourning for her, when he said, 'Do not weep any long, for she is not dead, but sleeping.' And they ridiculed him, because they knew that she was dead. But he took her by the hand and called to her, 'Child, arise!' Her breath returned and she immediately arose." New American Bible

Today's Prayer "Oh, Father, thank you, thank you, for it all. For the water so green and the sky so blue, I thank you. For children's laughter and love and joy, I thank you. For the fruit from the trees and the meal soon to be consumed, I thank you. You made it all and You give it away so freely to all. May I truly follow in Your example. Amen."

As expected, this morning the sun peeped out from behind a cloud, the wind blew, and birds sang. A large pod of dolphins swam outside the office window, with blows and squeals and little tails splashing. Observing it all, I paused to say, "Thank you, God, for Your many miracles." In the process of uttering these words I found a calm, a peace. God's spirit had entered mind and heart while my soul sang, "Another miracle, another miracle." All because of taking one brief thanksgiving moment, today I will be a fraction kinder, a tad gentler. It will take longer to lose my patience. And all the while, appreciating life and living, my soul sings, "Another miracle, another miracle."

Father, Son, and Holy Spirit = miracles.

Your life, my life = miracles.

Faith, steppingstones = miracles.

Come, join me in completing your list of miracles.

BE A BETTER PERSON
Reflection: Banking On The Memory Bank

Deposits and withdrawals. That is one description of the banking business. It is also a description of a human memory bank system. According to medical science and psychologists, nothing happens in our life that is not remembered. All moments are recorded. Most, however, are never recalled. So why are some memories recalled and others not? Personally, I believe that inside our brains is an area housing special memories. We selectively deposit memories through a "that's a keeper" preference process, just as we are the ones who decide when a memory is going to be withdrawn, given to God, or laid aside forever. Now here is the essential part of this entire networking system: The type of memories we keep help tell us what kind of person we are, plain and simple. Do we hold on to negative memories? Or do we primarily embrace happy memories?

If I believe myself to be a good and happy person, one who ultimately forgives and forgets, then the kept memories are going to be those which reflect this personal philosophy. If I know myself to be negative, looking for the worst, and believing that bad will happen, the kept memories will reflect life's dark and sad episodes.

In each person's life, memories will unexpectedly show themselves. A person or event reminds us of another time.

Deja vu strikes when hearing a certain tone, or experiencing a smell, a touch, or a sight. We have no control over these recalled memories. They hit without warning and can remind us of either a pleasant or unpleasant time in life. An unpleasant recall may either have been a keeper (we will talk about this next) or may be stored in our subconscious. A pleasant memory is from the 'keeper" file. We cherish our keeper" memories for these are the ones who accompany us into our senior years.

Now here is the whole point of this exercise: We want—and need—to be *happy* with a sense of well-being when older. We need to know we will smile a lot. Today, we need to make happy memories for this goal to become a reality.

What are you doing right now to guarantee yourself tomorrow's smiles from the happy memories made this day?

Scriptural Readings by Johnson & McCormick

Psalms 37.1-9 "Do not get heated about the wicked or envy those who do wrong. Quick as the grass they wither, fading like the green of the fields.

"Put your trust in Yahweh and do right, make your home in the land and live secure. Make Yahweh your joy and he will give you your heart's desires.

"Commit your destiny to Yahweh, be confident in him, and he will act, making your uprightness clear as daylight, and the justice of your cause as the noon.

"Stay quiet before Yahweh, wait longingly for him, do not get heated over someone who is making a fortune, succeeding by devious means.

"Refrain from anger, leave rage aside, do not get heated - it can do no good; for evil-doers will be annihilated, while those who hope in Yahweh shall have the land for their own." New Jerusalem Bible

Proverbs 10.7a "The memory of the just is blessed." King James Version

Today's Prayer "Dear Father, today I long to rack up happy keeper memories. Show me the way into Your heart so that our time will be filled with joy. On this day, together, may we know laughter and smiles aplenty. May we look together at the same sights and share the same experiences with gladness of heart. May Your kiss be felt upon my soul, filling it with love and glory, so that I may venture into the world and proclaim the happiness You have placed within. On this day, may I proclaim the keeper memory of Jesus standing on one side of me and the Holy Spirit on the other side. With this picture, I kneel before You. Amen."

BE A BETTER PERSON
Reflection: Why Have I Kept This "Bad" Memory?

The main flaw with the memory bank process is that it is not so neat and clean. Grossly negative people do have *good* memories and basically positive people can and do have some awful memories. These too, as hard as it is to believe, have many times also been selected as 'keepers'. It is easy to see why negative people would hold on to a few good memories for without them, these people would literally go crazy. Negativity can only blanket so much and then it is either severe depression or suicide. But why on earth would people with positive outlooks hold on to *bad* memories?

Primarily because bad memories and living through their aftermath are keepers of lessons learned. Painful experiences become badges earned from the training ground of life. No one is free from hurt and pain. We have all suffered. We all have not one, but many, many stories to tell. Using our *God-giving ability* to turn these hurtful, harmful lessons into Survival Pride allows us to grow far beyond the initial shock these experiences accorded our fragile senses.

A problem occurs when we refuse to let go of the encounter, when we steadfastly refuse to learn and grow from the experience. You have met such a person, the one who talks and talks and cries over the *incident*. S/he has the constant litany of "if only" and nothing great or fine has happened in life since *that awful* occurrence. Aside from our impatience, we end up pitying this individual.

Yet, is it not ironic, a contradiction, that we do not feel sorry for ourselves when we refuse to let go of a hurtful memory, a still-bearing pain?

We need to make time today to reflect upon what continues to hurt our body/mind/soul connection. We   begin by putting aside for later consideration the issues of a traumatic nature. Let us begin with lesser pain. Which awful memory shall we put to rest? What reoccurrence plagues our nightmares? What memory is of a longtime past and its people no longer part of our daily lives? What memory frustrates and tempts the yelling aloud "Enough is enough"?

Once this memory has been chosen, we take a good look at it. Give it the "microscope" treatment, leaving no nuance unexamined. When did this occur? In what environment (place)? What was the atmosphere like: hostile, gentle, everyday, expectant? Who were the players, even in minor roles? What was said? What was known but left unsaid? What were the vocal tones and how did they sound? What was the variety of expressions? What were feelings before, during and after? After ascertaining these answers, we are in the place of reliving the experience. Now answer truthfully to the following questions:

In what ways has this changed my life for the worse?

How many times have I turned away from this memory, allowing its fear and its hurt to keep me from doing, trying, or even be-ing?

Is this person (or those people) worth my happiness?

Where was God at the time this happened?

Did I recognize God's presence at the time?

Is its aftermath really worth all the time spent and all the agony felt?

Just once, what I have gained from thinking "if only"?

Admit now the time has come to let go. Ask our Father for this memory to be taken away. Once you have successfully done your work, God will grant your prayer.

If you find resistance, ask yourself this question: Is this worth my life's happiness, peace of mind? God does not want this for you and will help you be rid of it forever. Guaranteed.

Scriptural Readings by Johnson & McCormick

Psalm 94.17-19 "Unless the Lord had given me help, I would soon have dwelt in the silence of death. When I said, 'My foot is slipping,' your love, O Lord, supported me. When anxiety was great within me, your consolation brought joy to my soul." New International Version, The Living Insights Study Bible

Psalm 145 "God is here - let's celebrate! Let us enlist our lives in perpetual celebration over God's goodness and greatness. Let us announce to the world God's presence and proclaim His loving concern for all men.

"How compassionate He is over all He has created, how tender toward His failure-fraught creatures! He will not cop out on His promises to us. His blessings are not reserved only for those who fit obediently into His design for them. He is just - and He is forgiving. He gently picks up those who have fallen and restores them to sonship and servanthood. He sustains those who are wavering in weakness and grants them His grace and strength.

He reaches into the void of empty lives and enriches and fulfills their hungry hearts. He is near enough to hear our every cry, to sense our every need, to grant us whatever is necessary to make us happy and productive as we seek to follow and to serve Him. How incomparably glorious is our great God! May our mouths articulate, and our lives demonstrate His ever-present love for all His creatures. Let us celebrate the eternal mercy and goodness of our God." Psalms/Now

1Corinthians 15.1,2 "Now I would remind you, brethren, in what terms I preached to you the gospel, by which you are saved if you hold it fast." The Reader's Digest Bible

Today's Prayer "My Father, it is true that every time I allowed You to help me work through a bad memory, release and freedom has been the end result. Would You please explain to me then why I insist on holding on to _(the hurtful memory of choice)?_ At this point in my life, I would much rather just learn its needed lesson and get on with living. I am tired of being bogged down in the mire of bad feelings and old angers. Free me, dear Lord. Show me the steps! I want to be a Child of the Light, not this child of dark thought. With You is the life of peace—my goal—and Yours for me. Amen."

BE A BETTER PERSON
Reflection: No More Woxes

Don't you hate reading about yourself? Ruth Krauss wrote about me a very long time ago. And I so dislike seeing myself in print. She wrote, "There was a wolf and there was a fox, and they ate each other up. And that made a wox. Then the wox ate himself up and that's why there are no more waxes."

Once upon a time there was a BC who acted only to please other people and a BC who acted only to please herself. So much at odds at all times of the day and night, the two BCs finally merged into one self-centered, ego centric individual who finally drowned in a sea of "I", "me", "my way", "own", and "what's in it for me?" The drowning was slow—and very painful. The overblown ego began to dislike itself and despaired at having to hear the constant ego-talk. The "I's" finally went into oblivion.

Unlike the Phoenix, no new "BC" emerged completely cured of the I-ego. The battle of the wox ego versus God's Will is an ongoing struggle. This is not a battle of good versus evil for one's ego is hardly *evil*. It is more the case of wanting credit for good works, being told that the writing was "brilliant', and, "oh, my, what a good teacher you are. The class was highly interesting, and I can hardly wait till next Sunday!"

In Transactional Analysis terms these are called "strokes". We love our strokes and work hard for them. These are not God-strokes. They are people strokes that feed an unhealthy dependency.

God-strokes are not based upon deed but upon "be-ing". The reward from a God-stroke is far more powerful than any stroke given by a person or group. And they last a lot longer, too.

A God-stroke comes from deep within our souls, that place where we know we did a good job, took care of feelings and responsibilities, fulfilled obligations, and did so with maturity and kindness of heart. Knowing we have walked right with God fills our very being with a deep pleasure that easily brings a blush to one's own face. Unlike a people-stroke, a God-stroke nurtures, supports, and encourages. No sick symbiosis is grown here for dependence is not of health. But forgiveness and God's total forgetfulness over our imperfections and shortcomings are of health. There arrives a sense of wellbeing that comes from working for and with God. No human can offer such a gift, such a stroke. A God stroke is the faint-heard whisper "I am pleased with you."

Scriptural Readings by Johnson & McCormick

Luke 21.1-4 "He [Jesus] looked around and saw the rich folks putting their money into the collection plates. He noticed that a penniless widow put in two cents, and he said, 'It is surely true that this poverty-stricken widow put in more than the others, because all of them gave from their overflow, while she, from her scarcity, has put in all she has." The Cotton Patch Version of Luke and Acts

Revelation 21.3,4 "Then I heard a loud voice call from the throne, 'Look, here God lives among human beings. He will make his home among them; they will be his people, and he will be their God, God-with-them. He will wipe away all tears from their eyes; there will be no more death, and no more mourning or sadness or pain. The world of the past has gone." New American Bible

Today's Prayer "Only You, dear Jesus, know how deeply I long to be more like You. But, unfortunately, it is not only You who knows just how far I am from it! Every time I turn around there is the mirror's voice, and the friend's voice, and the enemy's voice, all too happily reciting my sins and shortcomings. At least You are kind in Your reminders of how I could have done better. Father instilled in my heart the picture of what Heaven's kingdom would look like here on Earth and You, my Lord, offer Your teaching to New Life. All I need to do is follow them and in so doing, my fragile ego will blend with God's Will.

"Holy Spirit, come, light my path so that I don't lose sight of Jesus' examples. Help me find healthy ways to combine ego with Divine Guidance so that we both might live in peace. Amen."

Pray this prayer with me. Keep them in your heart when wanting to boil with temper, or sidestep the truth, or commit the many wrongdoing available to all of us.

BE A BETTER PERSON
Reflection: You Are What You Eat? No, You Are What You Think!
Or I Deserve Everything I Get

Constant negative thoughts make for a constantly negative person. A person who thinks about death and dying all the time lives a half-dead life. And the person whose only intimacy is with money is a bankrupt person.

If the food I put—or don't—into my mouth makes me fat, thin, sick, or healthy, then do the thoughts that feed my heart turn me into a healthy and bright, or a dark and emotionally hurting individual. Unfortunately, I alone am in control of the food potions *and* the thought process. So much responsibility! Could not God have lightened up a little? Taken on more of the decisions?

Alas, no. Not if we are to possess Free Will.

During the desert trek, manna from heaven fed the people. Do we see pictures of fat people making this trek? No. Skinny and healthy they were. We don't read about disease or the need for operations during this forty-year walk. No. What we hear are the cries of boredom over lack of choice. The food is boring, the leaders are predictable and boring, and the never-ending trek is boring! Even God was boring. What had happened to all the sparkle, challenges, and zest of life? Gone.

So here is the bottom line: either God takes back a few of the Free Will choices aid leaves me with limited life decisions and lots of boredom or I can shut my mouth and turn off negativity and live a life of freedom of choice and responsibility.

Scriptural Readings by Johnson & McCormick

Deuteronomy 15.15 "Remember that you were once a slave in Egypt and that Yahweh your God redeemed you; that is why I am giving you this order today." New Jerusalem Bible

Psalm 119.105-109 "Your word is a lamp to my feet, a light on my path; I have bound myself by oath and solemn vow to keep your just decrees. I am cruelly afflicted; Lord, revive me as you have promised. Accept, Lord, the willing tribute of my lips and teach me your decrees. Every day I take my life in my hands, yet I never forget your law." Revised English Bible

Acts 14.21-23 "After they had proclaimed the good news to that city and made a considerable number of disciples, they returned to Lystra and to Iconium and to Antioch. They strengthened the spirits of the disciples and exhorted them to persevere in the faith, saying, 'It is necessary for us to undergo many hardships to enter the kingdom of God.' They appointed presbyters for them in each church and, with prayer and fasting, commended them to the Lord in whom they had put their faith." New American Bible

Today's Prayer "'How I praise You, 0 Lord, because You love me even when I fail to respond in loving obedience! Whereas I cannot comprehend You, You do understand me, and You continue to hold me within Your loving embrace. While I fall short of my sincere intentions to abide within Your will for me,

Your promises are eternally secure, and You tenderly and patiently rekindle the fires within me and empower me to do that which I cannot do by myself. I love You, 0 God, and I gladly accept Your will and purpose for my life. Now bless me and guide me and grant me the grace to walk within that will and purpose and have the joy of knowing that I am pleasing You. Amen."' (Note: These verses come from the book by Leslie F. Brandt called *Psalms/Now.* I turned it into a prayer as its words are most appropriate for today's study. BC)

Free Will is a God-gift of many consequences. How do you use this gift? Could you do better in its utilization? Could you do more?

BE A BETTER PERSON
Reflection: Surrounded By "Good" Friends

Many decades ago, a very wise lady and I had lunch together. Ida asked questions about my writing and then asked the most extraordinary question, "BC, just how many of your friends support your effort to be a Christian writer?"

I literally had to stop and think before I attempted to answer this rather simple question. At the time, most were more interested in how many pages were written each day than in their content, a condition of quantity over quality. I had to face the fact that I had people in my life who showed no interest in *reading* what I wrote. One such person said to me, "I love to tell my friends I hang with a writer." Another said, "I'd rather have you read it to me or just tell me about it." And yet another said, "Oh, you're good. I don't have to read it to know I'd like it." And one even had the nerve to question, "Do you *have to be* a Christian writer? Sex and violence sell so much easier!"

Ida went on to observe, "We hurt until we surround ourselves with people who truly have our best interest at heart. Deep inside we live with a core feeling of loneliness, and of never quite being understood to the depth we desire. When we try to stem these feelings, we often find ourselves reaching for the phone but never completing the call because we will stop to think, 'Now isn't a good time,' or, if we are honest, 'S/he won't really be interested.'"

Because Ida's point hit home, I realized change was needed. We hate dismantling our life, but sometimes it is necessary. When I smoked cigarettes, all my friends did likewise. When I dismissed God's importance, all my close friends were non-churched. My friends changed as this intimate spiritual journey with God deepened. Heeding Ida's important observation, I now surround myself with people who enjoy reading my works "hot off the printer". And friend Ida was absolutely right. The quality of life has enormously improved! I am a happier person, and certainly a more at-ease individual now that there are people around who support and encourage my deepest desire.

Today's job is to stay away from those who do not support who I am, who I am becoming, and where I want to go. God is in all of this for it is God who has helped me become today's person, and it is God who gave me the vision as to who I could grow into and is helping me become that individual.

Are you also on this all-important journey?

Scriptural Readings by Johnson & McCormick

Genesis 232.25-29 "It had been Jacob's intent to make a private crossing of the Jabbok. But maybe he trusted the swimming stroke of his strong arm better in daylight than in the dark; and maybe the night fell faster within the walls of the gorge than he had expected. Whatever the reason, he did not dive into the waters. He did not move. He stood transfixed, surrounded by sound and soon by an absolute darkness - for even the tiny stars were suddenly swallowed as if by a beast of horrible size.

"Jacob felt wind, then a chill.

"Someone came flying down the riverbank. Jacob felt what he could not see. Then someone attacked him, struck him to the stony ground, and began to wrestle with him. They wrestled by the river. They whirled and heaved each other against the sheer rock wall. In a breathless silence they wrestled all night until a high gray dawn began to streak the sky.

"Jacob's adversary touched him in the hollow of his thigh and put his thigh out of join.

"Jacob threw his arm around a huge waist and held on.

"The massive foe said, 'Let me go, for the day is breaking.' But Jacob shouted, 'I will not let you go, unless you bless me.'

"'What is your name?' '"Jacob.'

"'The contender said, 'Your name shall no more be called Jacob, but Israel, for you have striven with God and with men, and have prevailed.'" The Book of God

1Thessalonians 2.1. 5-9 "You yourselves know, brothers and sisters, that our coming to you was not in vain."

"As you know and as God is our witness, we never came with words of flattery or with a pretext for greed; nor did we seek praise from mortals, whether from you or from others, though we might have made demands as apostles of Christ. But we were gentle among you, like a nurse tenderly caring for her own children. So deeply do we care for you that we are determined to share with you not only the gospel of God but also our own selves, because you have become very dear to us." New Revised Standard Version

Today's Prayer "Dear Jesus, You know so much better than I just how hard it is to find people who will support visions, dreams, and lessons. You did not want to entertain with Your healings and teachings, but to instruct. You never wanted to be lied against, mocked, or left to fend on Your own, but You were. And You endured it all out of love for our Father. You left childhood behind, the town, friends, even family. You left behind those who knew You as a teenager and as a young adult. You were called into our Father's work and gathered around those who would support this endeavor. Teach me, Lord, how to do the same. Those people who can only see who I was yesterday cannot be a friend of who I am today."

"In Your love, I shall not be lonely."

"With Your support, I shall indeed be strong."

"Thank you for teaching me through Your examples. Amen."

BE A BETTER PERSON
Reflection: A Frustrating Relationship, Part 1

If you like pelicans and if you like the seagull, then you are not going to like this story. Don't get me wrong. I like them fine. Pelicans dive into the water outside the condo windows all day long. Some are gray headed, some have yellow heads, and once I saw an all-white pelican who was marvelous to watch as he soared through the Florida pale blue sky. His huge wings kept disappearing against the low billowing white-grayish clouds.

I have the same liking for seagulls. How could one not what with so many colors, varieties, and shapes. Their spindly legs are delightful to watch as they bend backwards and run, holding a weight that looks like it would crush them. Their long, skinny beaks are razor sharp and bring respect for the way they can dashingly pierce through their next meal.

It is the relationship a seagull will form with a pelican that I find frustrating. The soaring pelican spots his meal and swoops into the ocean, his head disappearing beneath the water. His head emerges but he leaves his beak underwater for a moment. Slowly, very slowly, he brings his fish-filled beak out of the water. With a quick flare, he tosses back his head and one can see fish being swallowed, the bulge swelling his neck for a brief instant.

There swims the seagull, right next to the pelican. He is too far away so he inches closer still until, to the onlooker, they appear as one form. Not satisfied, he flies up to the pelican's head just as it is emerging from the water. The seagull squats, riding with it as it bobs out of water and into the air. The seagull watches the pelican's beak. There! Look! Water drains rapidly from the beak's side slots. The seagull observes the stunned minnows and shiners flowing out!

"Food!" screams the seagull as he jumps into the water, swooping up the dead and dying fish.

I bet you too have a two-legged seagull hanging around, waiting to claim your hard work as his or her own. Now why do we, like the pelicans, allow this subservient relationship to exist?

Scriptural Readings by Johnson & McCormick

Genesis 25.19-34 "Now these are the begettings of Yitzhak (Isaac), son of Avraham. Avraham begot Yitzhak. Yitzhak was forty years old when he took Rivka (Rebekah) daughter of Betuel the Aramean, from the country of Aram, sister of Lavan the Aramean, for himself as a wife. Yitzhak entreated YHWH on behalf of his wife, for she was barren, and YHWH granted-his-entreaty: Rivka his wife became pregnant. But the children almost crushed one another inside her, so she said: If this is so, why do I exist? And she went to inquire of YHWH. YHWH said to her: Two nations are in your body, two tribes from your belly shall be divided; tribe shall be mightier than tribe, elder shall be servant to younger!

"When the days were fulfilled for bearing, there: twins were in her body! The first one came out ruddy, like a hairy mantle all over, so they called his name: Esav (Esau)/Rough-One. After that his brother came out, his hand grasping Esav's heel, so they called his name: Yaakov (Jacob)/Heel Holder.

"Yitzhak was sixty years old when she bore them. The lads grew up: Esav became a man who knew the hunt, a man of the field, but Yaakov was a plain man, staying among the tents. Yitzhak grew to love Esav, for (he brought) hunted-game for his mouth, but Rivka loved Yaakov.

"Once Yaakov was boiling boiled-stew, when Esav came in from the field, and he was weary. Esav said to Yaakov: Pray give me a gulp of the red stuff, that red-stuff, for I am so weary! Therefore they called his name: Edom/Red One.

"Yaakow said: Sell me your firstborn-right her-and-now. Esav said: Here, I am on my way to dying, so what good to me is a firstborn-right? Yaakow said: Swear to me here-and-now. He swore to him and sold his firstborn right to Yaakov.

"Yaakov gave Esav bread and boiled lentils; he ate and drank and arose and went off. Thus did Esav despise the firstborn-right." The Five Books of Moses

NOTE: If I agreed with the premise that the pelican and seagull are caught in some sort of destructive symbiosis - which I don't - I would offer the following readings. Actually, I offer the reading as an example of one who claims the work of another, which this story is obviously about. Rev. DJ

2Kings 3.21-23 "When the Moabites learned that the kings were advancing to fight them, all those of an age to bear arms were mobilized; they took up position on the frontier.

In the morning when they got up, the sun was shining on the water; and in the distance the Moabites saw the water as red as blood. This is blood!' they said. The kings must have fought among themselves and killed one another. So now for the booty, Moab!" New Jerusalem Bible

Today's Prayer "Dear Lord, I do try to keep one step ahead of my enemies. Rarely does a day goes by that someone isn't trying to make trouble through lies, jealousy, or meanness. I try hard, God, I really do, to turn the other cheek but I must be honest and say there are times when I find it impossible to do so. How do I let another take credit for the work I do? How do I allow someone to claim my idea as his or her own? How am I supposed to do this when my very job or promotion or relationship may rest upon the fact that this is my work?

"It is one thing to read Your Word, God, and another to ive by it. I don't want to fail either You or myself. I see and accept myself as a Child of the Resurrection and the anger or the burning desire to *get even* has no place in this picture. Help me, Spirit of God, to tread lightly and righteously, doing the Will of my Father. Help me to trust that God will right the wrong without any interference or influence from me. So easy to pray, so hard to live. But because my desire to not fail You is more important than any momentary earthly concern, I shall guard my tongue, walk away, and leave this in Your divine hands. Amen."

NOTE: Communications are so much fun. I write "subservient relationship" and Doris writes "destructive symbiosis". I believe them to have different meanings, but on reflection, maybe both work in this reflection. What is important is that no matter what relationship we are involved with, it is healthy for both parties.

Are your relationships on an even keel? No one-upmanship going on? Respect flowing, ideas and laughter shared? If not, can the relationship be healed? Talking things out, expression of how you really feel, will help.

BE A BETTER PERSON

Reflection: Sometimes What We Think We See Just Isn't So; Or A Frustrating Relationship, Part 2

The system of compiling this little book was established early—I write the Reflection, make two copies, giving one each to Reverends Johnson and McCormick. They would identify scripture, return their work to me, and I would type it up. Viola! All finished. Except this one time. On the "A Disgusting Relationship" article, I received back scribbled notes from Doris, talking about symbiosis.

Well, I had to stop and think. All along something was troublesome about my conclusion. I had yet to discover answers to these questions: Why were the pelicans so passive about seagulls landing on their heads? Why didn't they at least try to shake them off? Where was their righteous anger? They certainly were entitled to it. After all, who wants parasites hanging around? Not seeing any other angle to the picture, I concluded that pelicans are stupid creatures, not worth all this thought.

Wrong thinking. Wrong conclusion.

As Rev. Doris pointed out, another way to look at their relationship is one of cooperation. The pelicans already knew they were not going to mess with the small stuff, those tiny fish that spew out in the overflow of their beaks. Why not share their bounty, excess, with another? Why shouldn't their labor ease the life of another? Is this not something our Lord calls us to do in everyday?

What I have yet to figure out is the seagulls landing on top of the pelican's head. Now that must hurt—their sharp claws digging into the pelican's head! Or, at least, be uncomfortable. But I am going to have to wait until another friend comes along to explain the rationale behind this behavior.

What Doris did for me is a part of friendship, the healthy part of any relationship. She asked me to stretch, to consider another point of view. I could have easily fought for my conclusion. Nothing says I must change my mind. But is it not exciting to share differences of opinion, differences in view, without getting hung up in ego? Isn't it grand to have such a friend who will say, "But wait, let's consider this—."

Two things are of importance here: one, it is essential to keep open both mind and heart so that another's viewpoint may be heard *and* felt. It doesn't really matter whether I believe the new information or not. It does not matter if I see the term "symbiosis" in a different light. What is important is that it is heard and thought about. This ability to listen and sometimes change is also an ingredient in respect for others and for self. Second, it is vital to have people in our lives that offer differences of opinion and who stretch our perspectives, awareness, and viewpoints.

Are you open to diverse opinions?

Scriptural Readings by Johnson & McCormick

Numbers 5.10 "Whatever anyone consecrates is his own; whatever is given to the priest belongs to the priests."

(NOTE: The reading for the pelican/seagull that comes to my mind is Jesus' flogging at the hands of the crowd on his way to the cross. The reading for the response to that passage is 'let those with ears to hear, and eyes to see ... do it!' Rev DJ)

Luke 23.13-25 "Pilate then summoned the chief priests, the rules, and the people and said to them, 'You brought this man to me and accused him of inciting the people to revolt. I have conducted my investigation in your presence and have not found this man guilty of the charges you have brought against him, nor did Herod, for he sent him back to us. So no capital crime has been committed by him. Therefore I shall have him flogged and then release him.'

"But all together they shouted out, 'Away with this man! Release Barabbas to us.' (Now Barabbas had been imprisoned for a rebellion that had taken place in the city and for murder.) Again Pilate addressed them, still wishing to release Jesus, but they continued their shouting, 'Crucify him! Crucify him!' Pilate addressed them a third time, 'What evil has this man done! I found him guilty of no capital crime. Therefore I shall have him flogged and then release him.' With loud shouts, however, they persisted in calling for his crucifixion, and their voices prevailed. The verdict of Pilate was that their demand should be granted. So he released the man who had been imprisoned for rebellion and murder, for whom they asked, and he handed Jesus over to them to deal with as they wished."
New American Bible

Today's Prayer "God of All, life sometimes gets crazy. Too many times throughout the day I get the impression that we talk to one another but not with one another. We are too busy formulating our own thoughts to clearly hear each another, and we are so anxious to speak that we talk right through another's words without really understanding the impact of their speech. I need to hear from other people, Lord. Otherwise, I have only my own opinions to go by and we know how erroneous that can be! To hear others, I need to develop the habit of listening first, thinking it through second, and third, well, then it's my turn.

Gracious God, I ask that You continue to bring good people into my life who will reinforce reasoning with debate and who have different perspectives and are willing to share their thoughts. I know that while stopping to hear and think, I will find Your Presence. The people who cause me to stop and think and help me understand the complexes of life and faith are intricate parts of my spiritual journey toward You. I thank you for them, dear Lord. Amen."

BE A BETTER PERSON
Reflection: The Fishhook

Ever been given a promise that was not kept?

Ever have a date broken - more than once, by the same person?

Ever waited around for the person to show up, only s/he never did?

Ever listen in long silence to the phone that never rang?

Ever sit alone in a restaurant, pretending to be busy writing/reading/thinking   because the chair across from you remains empty?

Ever have one hour become six hours or one day become a week?

Ever sit in a meeting where a hidden agenda was being played out and you and the others belatedly realize you are just being led down the path?

Ever been lied to so that you would or would not—.

Ever have the same person, over and over, make commitments of change and never carry though?

Ever feel like a fish that keeps on swallowing the same line and hook over and over and over?

Since we all are guilty of being such a fish, sometimes passively waiting to be jerked first this way and then that way, or sometimes fighting for dear life, with deflated egos, we need to stop and ask ourselves, "Why?"

Scriptural Readings by Johnson & McCormick

Passivity: When we go through these experiences we are suffering from a loss of who we are and who (God) is the center of our life. I see as the response to this commitment to our own basic truth (finding our basic truth should be the quest of life, but too often we leave this in the hands of another). Think of the verse below where the ultimate question becomes: Do you want to be healed? P.M.

John 5.5-13 "Later on Jesus went up to Jerusalem for one of the Jewish festivals. Now at the Sheep-Pool in Jerusalem there is a place with five colonnades. Its name in the language of the Jews is Bethesda. In these colonnades there lay a crowd of sick people, blind, lame, and paralysed. Among them was a man who had been crippled for thirty-eight years. When Jesus saw him lying there and was aware that he had been ill a long time, he asked him, 'Do you want to recover?'

"Sir,' he replied, 'I have no one to put me in the pool when the water is disturbed, but while I am moving, someone else is in the pool before me.'

Jesus answered, 'Rise to your feet, take up your bed and walk.' The man recovered instantly, took up his stretcher, and began to walk.

"That day was a Sabbath. So the Jews said to the man who had been cured, 'It is the Sabbath. You are not allowed to carry your bed on the Sabbath.' He answered, 'The man who cured me said, "take up your bed and walk."' They asked him, 'Who is the man who told you to take up your bed and walk?' But the cripple who had been cured did not know; for the place was crowded and Jesus had slipped away." The New English Bible

Ephesians 4.25 "Then have done with falsehood and speak the truth to each other, for we belong to one another as parts of one body."
Revised English Bible

Today's Prayer "Dear Lord, why do I allow others to control my life? Why do I wait when I *know* it is not forthcoming? Why do I believe when I *know* it's a lie? Why don't I speak up when I *know* the game is in play? How can I ever respect myself if I continue to allow this abuse? Oh, God, You didn't put me on this earth to be abused. You do give me the knowledge to know when it is happening and, with Your help and guidance, I will find ways to stop it, to walk away, or simply ignore the lies and get on with my life. Thank you, Lord, for these insights and guidance which help me grow closer to You. Amen."

Abused, being taken advantage of, lies come streaming in, history being retold in ways that does not benefit you or show you in a good light? Yes, this happens, sadly, to most everyone. The important thing is not to be sucked into the turmoil. Do not play the game. No words. Walk away. Trust me, not worth your time or energy. Learn, as a person of Faith, to protect yourself against gaming. Your silence is your best friend. Going down to someone else's level is your worst enemy. What warning, key, can you give yourself to know that now is not the time to involve yourself?

BE A BETTER PERSON
Reflection: The Awakening

Once, I was in Sally's company for long periods of time. Now, it was going to happen again. Since we had not seen one another in a long time, on the surface, the day's outing sounded like a good idea. The biggest hurdle to overcome is how, every time in the past that I saw her, I promised myself the visit would be different, but it never was. I always promised I would react differently to her words, to her actions. Still, now that I've made this commitment again, I wonder, how long before it happens again?

You, too, are familiar with this relationship strife as it has many forms and is expressed in a variety of hidden agendas: poutiness, over-the-line self centeredness, anger, sweet-to-sour-to-sweet personality, overt manipulation, scorn, ridicule, bringing up the past, and bringing up subject matters that hurt. And, of course, the one used most often, that of passive-aggressive behavior. This one really hits the *hot* button.

Sadly, by evening's end, I discovered none of my "changes of behavior" worked. I still reacted to Sally the same as I did years earlier. By this evening's end, I was ready to abandon this relationship. Like most people, I resent the feeling of being a puppet whose strings are yanked, stretched, and pulled. Why would anyone, I asked myself throughout the long day, deliberately and continually push another person's buttons to elicit frustration, irritation, anger, and eventually, reach the ultimate goal of rage or tears?

Silly question. It is all a matter of control over another person. The simple and painful truth is that I hand her the power to manipulate my emotions and hand her the control to go from one destructive word or action to another. From experience, I learned that giving in stops a lot of fights. Those pro-longed discussions end up doing what she wanted to do anyway. So why bother? In self-disgust, but silent, I literally place myself upon the altar, a sacrificial lamb. Just like in the feeding of the pagan gods, I allow myself to be used as fodder to feed the destructive need of another.

I have known for years that my friend Sally has problems. However, in today's world of abuse and insecurity her problems are not unique. As a result of her past, my friend distrusts the love and forgiveness offered within the Christian faith. She dislikes and disbelieves any form of goodness found in my behavior. As a Christian, I am no different—and certainly no better—than she and this Sally sets out to prove.

This last time her game was replayed. I, again, became helpless and failed at any new behavior. Frustrated, down on myself, and in ignorance, I only knew the uncomfortable feeling of being trapped in her control had happened again. It wasn't until evening when, with great clarity, I saw the look of immense satisfaction on her face. A deep knowledge fell into place. She knew I was on the edge, as angry as I had ever been.

"There," said the thoughts so readable in her eyes, "by your actions and words, you are no better than me. As a matter of fact, I am superior because I would never let myself be controlled by another as you have!"

My weakness gave her affirmation that neither God nor Jesus's lessons have value. If Jesus's disciples react the same way as other motley groups of unbelievers, then her superiority in not buying into the "Great Falsehood" is justified.

That moment of clarity was a spiritual slap in my face. I had vowed to cease being a victim, yet so readily I handed myself over. Why? Because I do not want to argue or because it is easier to let her have her own way or because it takes too much time and effort to assert myself? Am I so insecure and so desirous of being liked that I sell out my Faith? I know of no case where Jesus 'went along'. I can recall no incident where our Lord made time a precedent over a person. Nowhere in the New Testament does it show where Jesus rolled over or gave His power to another so that He did not have to be responsible. Jesus' life and teachings are examples of sharing, of bringing out the best in one another. This friend and I are in the worse kind of dysfunctional relationship.

I can dissolve this relationship. After all, it is only an investment in years that did not pay off. And because it is *just* a friendship, I can call it quits. Quitting is not an option when it is family or a manipulative boss from whom I need the job. Yet, in truth, I cannot quit on this friendship either, not if I claim Christendom as my Faith, my life. This is not a matter of "I'll show her Christ is the answer" but a matter of how Jesus led by example and how I must do the same.

I will pray for Sally, even if in the beginning the words sound empty to my ears. With God's grace, in time, meaning will grow behind those words. And I will be kind to her without relinquishing personal power. This will be the hard part, to not react to stings and to maintain control in face of manipulative gestures. I will love Sally as I love myself and I will forgive her of all wrongdoing just as I pray God will forgive me of my sins. Truly, what I do in this relationship will affect and effect other aspects of my life. Growing strong, loving, and more Christlike will enable me to do the same with others. Before I depended upon my own strength, ego, and determination. Failing has taught me the need to do this in concert with my Faith. With my eye on God, I can do this. With my eye on God, the dysfunction will be destroyed, and Sally and I will find our way into a healthy relationship.

Do you have a "Sally" or "Sam" in your life where you need to change your mind and behavior towards?

Scriptural Readings by Johnson & McCormick

John 9.1-5 "As he went along, he saw a man who had been blind from birth. His disciples asked him, 'Rabbi, who sinned, this man or his parents, that he should have been born blind?'

"'Neither he nor his parents sinned,' Jesus answered, 'he was born blind so that the works of God might be reveal in him.

"'As long as day lasts we much carry out the work of the one who sent me; the night will soon be here when no one can work. As long as I am in the world I am the light of the world.'" New Jerusalem Bible

2Peter 2.11-12 "Dear friends, you are only visitors here. Since your real home is in heaven I beg you to keep away from the evil pleasures of this world; they are not for you, for they fight against your very souls. Be careful how you behave among your unsaved neighbors; for then, even if they are suspicious of you and talk against you, they will end up praising God for your good works when Christ returns." The Jesus Book

Today's Prayer "God, today I have an unusual prayer. I need You to give me a dose of insight and clarity and then the strength to act on the perceptiveness You offer. Your Son walked this earth giving examples of what it means for us to be Your son, Your daughter. Because I am a lover of Jesus, I too am called to live a life of Christian example and, sometimes, I make a terrible mess of it. Today I pray for the Spirit to act as an inhibitor, causing me to slow down and think more while acting less so that I might receive

Your gifts of clarity and insight. And let me not run from any truth, dear Lord, that is not to my liking but to stand strong and do my Father's Will. It is very difficult for me to be kind yet firm and to love a person I do not always like. Yet, I know You are my Light and my Strength. With You, I can and will do the hard work of change. Amen."

BE A BETTER PERSON
Reflection: It's All In The Attitude

Society continues to suffer consequences from life in the late 80s through the 90s. A now older "I" generation thinks, plans, and acts on a motto which became entrenched during this period, and it influences the actions or non-actions of our new millennium culture. "What's in it for me?" is more than a trend, a fad. It affects relationships and is reflected in the underlying philosophy of all institutions and their programs. If, how, and why a person worships heads the list of all institutions for society is affected by this one question. Here are just a few observations on how the church institution has changed over the last 20 years:

- Elders, council or chapter members, and vestry serve because it "looks good on the resume". You may add your own "many" or "most" or "few" members.
- Kitchens with large dining areas are now considered essential for any church building. If members tend to be creative, there will be a membership drop or difficulty in membership gain for members break bread at the altar and at the table, both purposes now serving a necessary function.
- "Pews" are old fashioned. Comfortable seats are a must and so are "breaks" and "refreshments".
- Holy Bible studies now take place in the form of entertaining Holy Bible stories.

- Theatrical productions and professional musicians and singers help define "worship", especially on holy days; excuse me, Holidays.
- Classes and presenters need to be entertaining first and informative, second.
- Once funerals were personal affairs where pastors intimately knew the deceased and family and could relate wonderful stories based upon this friendship.
- World Series, Playoffs, and tournaments come but once a year and have priority.

I reflect on how this has changed from childhood days. Families went to church on Sunday. Malls were not open, the Blue Laws were in effect, and soccer games were not played. Sundays belonged to God, church, family, and friends, in that order. This was a time when children memorized prayers and knew firsthand the names and struggles of biblical characters. Teens knew the books of the Holy Bible by order while young people could quote verses by the dozen and sing as many songs as possible without the need of a choir. Adults knew the prayers by heart. They could also tell you, without long thought, why they believed in Jesus and why they were members of this denomination.

So, I complain to God. And God convicts me with this: While I have not been guilty of all the above, I am guilty of these: Sometimes the weather is too cold or the rain too hard, or the sun and temperature are too hot, so I stay home. Sometimes I do not want to be around people, so I stay home. Sometimes I get tired of hearing about money concerns or the need for volunteers, so I stay home. It is also true that sometimes I would rather laugh and talk, than listen. And I would rather be entertained than need to think. I certainly would rather someone else supply the answers than be called upon to offer possible solutions or insights!

Then God sends this final word: "If I am unhappy that many people no longer attend church except as C&E's, and if I am unhappy the church bends over backwards to please in order to get people to attend, who do I think helped cause the problem?"

Oh, oh, with my attitude, did I add to these problems?

Scriptural Readings by Johnson & McCormick

Psalms 139.23,24 "Search me, 0 God, and know my heart; test me and know my thoughts. See if there is any wicked way in me, and lead me in the way everlasting." New Revised Standard Version

Mark 10.17-24 "As he was starting out on a trip, a man came running to him and knelt down and asked, 'Good Teacher, what must I do to get to heaven?'

"'Why do you call me good?' Jesus asked. 'Only God is truly good! But as for your question - you know the commandments: don't kill, don't commit adultery, don't steal, don't lie, don't cheat, respect your father and mother.'

"'Teacher,' the man replied, 'I've never once broken a single one of those laws.'

"Jesus felt genuine love for this man as he looked at him. 'You lack only one thing,' he told him; 'go and sell all you have and give the money to the poor - and you shall have treasure in heave - and come, follow me.'

"Then the man's face fell, and he went sadly away, for he was very rich. Jesus watched him go, then turned around and said to his disciples, 'It's almost impossible for the rich to get into the

Kingdom of God!' This amazed them. So Jesus said it again: 'Dear children, how hard it is for those who trust in riches to enter the Kingdom of God.'" The Jesus Book

Today's Prayer "Lord, have You noticed how quick I am to judge others? They have many flaws and faults You know, and I always experience this wonderful sense of self-righteousness when I begin to list how wrong *they* are. For shame that they—but then I usually get no further for You are there, standing before me and asking, "They?" No, Lord, not 'they' or 'them' but 'me'. Forgive me, God, for I too look for ways to entice and modernize, sometimes just for the sake of change, making 'new' and increasing numbers. You and The Word almost take a backseat. It is somewhat like trying to sneak You in through the backdoor. I do not want to be like this, Lord. I will let others do what they feel they need to do, without my criticism or judgement, if no wrongdoing is being committed. What others feel is necessary is their own business. As for me, I will put You first and cease looking for the 'fun' and 'entertainment' and 'instant gratification'. This does not mean overly serious or without smiles and joy as these are byproducts of Your love. It does mean being more focused on You and less on 'them'. This will certainly be a nice change. Thank You, Lord, for this insight and inspiration. Amen."

To blame another, or a whole group of others is so much easier than looking in the mirror. The Christian Faith is in trouble. Church doors are closed due to lack of members. Too many unsavory people are serving behind the altar. Money is discussed far too often from the pulpit. Choosing which Holy Bible verses should be adhered to while ignoring the ones we don't like is a common course of action.

These are problems our Faith faces, and so many more. My part and your part are to help change this picture by being—day in and day out—the person of Faith our Lord calls us to be.

What change will you make that can actually make a difference?

BE A BETTER PERSON
Reflection: Lead Me In The Path Of Righteousness

For breakfast: sweet rolls or fruit and granola?

For dress: skirt above or below, pants loose or tight? For traffic: road rage or safety?

For office: work or play?

For co-worker: regard or flirtation? For boss: deference or gossip?

Person's sex: intolerance, bias or neutral?

Person's sexual orientation: stereotype or open-minded?

Person's skin color: bigotry or colored blind? Person's religion: prejudice or acceptance? Person's age: discrimination or respect?

Person's habits: scorn or tolerance?

Person's opinions: close-minded or interested? For Lunch: drink or salad?

Off-colored jokes: snicker or avoidance? Conversations: boring or purposeful? Argue or share?

Lifestyle: stuck or challenging?

Home: pigsty, harried or neat? Finances: debt or budget?

One's own children: frustration or pride? Self-improvement: lazy or encouraged? Self-image: discouraged or enhanced?

Books, magazines, radio, videos, movies, rap, TV shows: sexual, violent, titillating, or entertaining, educational?

Sunday mornings: sleep in, play or worship? Follow God or ?

Scriptural Readings by Johnson & McCormick

Matthew 6.9b-13   "Our Father in heaven,
hallowed be your name, your kingdom come, your will be done
on earth as it is in heaven.
Give us today our daily bread Forgive us our debts,
As we also have forgiven our debtors.
And lead us not into temptation, But deliver us from evil."
New International Version, The Living Insights Study Bible

1Corinthians 10.12-13   "If you think you are standing firm, take care, or you may fall. So far you have faced no trial beyond human endurance; God keeps faith and will not let you be tested beyond your powers, but when the test comes he will at the same time provide a way out and so enable you to endure." Revised English Bible

Today's Prayer "Father, when Jesus walked this earth He gave people a choice: Follow or not. Simple? In broad concept, yes, but living it day by day, no, not simple at all. Our world is less about You and more about now, New Age, and instant gratification.

It is impossible to not be influenced. My eyes and ears take it all in even as my heart cries out 'no'. You call us to be in this world but not of this world and this path of righteousness is very difficult. I fail more often than I succeed. Forgive my stumbles, dear Lord. My lack of courage and lack of discipline in refusing temptation serves no one, less of all You. I pray that the Holy Spirit will help keep me from wandering away and that angels' whispers will help me discern Your Will along The Way. My soul longs to be in righteousness for You are eternal while life is but a fleeting moment. Guard my ways, Lord, so that I am right with You and in You. Amen."

Choices and decisions all day long! It never changes. The demands call to us. We need to remember that Jesus slept, ate, and prayed. He did not neglect any aspect that was important to healthy living. We get overrun when we skip sleep, meals, and talking with God.

Do you have a schedule for your healthy living? Because life is always in flex, maybe it is time to make changes to your schedule.

BE A BETTER PERSON
Reflection: The Art Of Gift-Giving

We are a gift-giving people. We give pre-birth shower gifts, birth gifts, birthday gifts, graduation gifts beginning with nursery school all the way up to college graduation, and then there are wedding shower gifts, wedding gifts, and anniversary gifts. Also, we give or exchange gifts during some holidays such as Christmas, Valentines, and Easter. Add to this now rather lengthy gift-giving list the blended family with all its step-relations.

So, we buy or create, and package our gift in pretty paper and bows. Oh, and let us not forget the card. Special cards can cost as much as the present but hey, it's only money!

Wait a minute. There are gifts that cost nothing and yet mean everything. They come from the heart, are biblical, and are on the verge of becoming a lost art. The Gospel According to Acts tells of our church's beginnings where most of the laity were poor. They pooled their resources and, in this manner, cared for the widows and orphans. Nobody went without necessities, but these new Christians had other gifts of equal importance. They gave the

gifts of charity
gifts of generosity
gifts of kindness

It was not important that the gift-giver be known or identified. People cheerfully lent a hand to one another because they wanted to. Today, we have established Acts of Random Kindness Clubs with matching T-shirts and coffee mugs. How much further away can one get that society has to prompt its citizens to be kind to one another! Rarely do we find people who give gifts for the sheer joy of giving. Rarely do we experience people who, without fuss or even much thought, make offerings simply as an unspoken gesture as part of our Christian formation.

Many Sundays ago, I was reminded of the importance of our non-cost Christian gift giving. It was a schizophrenic morning where my brain was trying to satisfy a teaching urge, a writing urge, and serve God urge. My body was moving instinctively by brain-fog! I hurriedly returned to the altar because of an unlit candle and left the processional cross behind. Oh, oh, the music started, and everyone is waiting for the Crucifer—me! I hurried back to the Cross being held by a lady who quickly put it in my hands. I took it and began to turn to the altar, ready to lead the procession.

"Well, *thank you!*"came a growling reminder of the unsaid appreciation. The phrase dripped with scorn from the lady handing me the Cross, waiting to extract her pound of flesh for not receiving due payment. I stopped, one foot in mid-air, turned, eyes wide and said, "Oh, yes, thank you." But these words were never heard. Instead, I looked into eyes that were saying, "gotcha".

Two thoughts crossed my mind as I led the Cross to the altar. First, that even in church we seem to have a hard time being generous to one another and second, that God's call to acts of kindness and generosity have been polluted with rudeness and power plays. How sad that playing on people's distractions, problems, troubles, can help another feel superior.

To be able to say, "that person is not as good as me" or "that person is no better than I" truly pollutes God's kingdom here, now, with insidious meanspiritness.

I would like to be able to judge this woman harshly, but I cannot for I have been guilty of such wrongdoing. Every day offers opportunities to commit "random acts of kindness" and too many times, too busy, too caught up in our own self-important affairs, we waltz right on by. Even the common courtesy of "thank you" gets left behind.

If I had been an outsider, observing that little church interaction, I would have walked away muttering, "I am sure glad I'm not her." The problem is, looking back I wonder which one I would be talking about, the lady or myself.

Which say you?

Scriptural Readings by Johnson & McCormick

Mark 12.41-44 "Once he was standing opposite the temple treasury, watching as people dropped their money into the chest. Many rich people were giving large sums. Presently there came a poor widow who dropped in two tiny coins, together worth a farthing. He called his disciples to him.

"'I tell you this,' he said: 'this poor widow has given more than any of the others; for those others who have given had more than enough, but she, with less than enough, has given all that she had to live one.'" The New English Bible

1Peter 4.7-10 "The end of all things is at hand. Therefore, be serious and sober for prayers. Above all, let your love for one another be intense, because love covers a multitude of sins.

Be hospitable to one another without complaining. As each one has received a gift, use it to serve one another as good stewards of God's varied grace." New American Bible

Today's Prayer "Father, it would not have taken a second to say 'thank you' or 'I'm sorry' or 'how can I help'. But I did not say these as I should have today. Instead, I got caught up in the acts of accomplishing and striking through the 'things to do' list. I am not sure when it got into my head that it takes time to be nice, time to be gracious, time to be generous, time to be considerate. None of it is true. And, truly, it takes a lot more time trying to counteract the lapse. Holy One, instill back into my heart the God-given gifts that use to come naturally, without thought. That is the person I long to return to. That is the person I was when first embracing Jesus and beginning our walk together. I regret having moved away and pray with all my heart to return. Amen."

PROLOGUE

In these readings, did you notice how each day's life situation had not one but two or more biblical passages relating to its message or circumstances? The Holy Bible does that for us. Everything under the sun is literally covered in this most meaningful book of all books.

Even though the Holy Bible is a book of antiquity, it is not an outdated book. One of the reasons the Holy Bible is still internationally outselling all other books is because people around the world realize that this book is *alive*. It lives within anyone who reads and accepts. It lives within anyone who reads, says "no way" but continues to question. The Holy Bible talks to us, with us. The Holy Bible prays with us, for us. The Holy Bible is the most marvelous collection of books in all creation because it is a story about us, beginning in a time when brutally was still a way of life: "You hurt a member of my tribe; I will kill your entire tribe!" Then, Moses and the Ten Statements arrived. Animalism and primitive thinking died out as humanism took form. It took centuries to get to where we are. We are still in the process of transition because we, humanity, still have a long, long way to go.

To help us, questions will be answered by the Holy Bible. If you have a problem, the Holy Bible can guide you toward a resolution. If you need immediate help, the Holy Bible explains how that is attainable. The Holy Bible is a guide for Holy daily living.

Many translations are used in this book to expose you to the variety available in the marketplace. Also, popular today is single-focused Holy Bibles, those stressing certain themes, such as women's studies or Black heritage Holy Bibles. You may be requested to study from a specific translation while involved in a particular study. Nevertheless, find a Holy Bible that 'talks to you' and claim it as your own. The book that speaks to us is the one we will return to over and over for its wisdom and instruction. Books that bore us or are confusing due to style or language are not used. This is not for you. Make a friend of God's book and allow it the privilege of talking to you in the language, rhythm, and style you will enjoy.

Put the Holy Bible to good use in your life. You will not be sorry. The Holy Bible is your friend, just waiting for your attention. It will tell you things you never dreamed possible. It will tell you stories that will shock, surprise, and bring you to tears. It will tell you about yourself and show you ways to look anew at the person who looks back in the mirror. Importantly, the Holy Bible will explain the meaning of life and share the reason why you live. The more attention and thought and study you give the Holy Bible the more it will grow inside you. It is a great journey. Do not deny yourself the privilege or the joy. The Holy Bible will change your life forever.

May God's blessing be upon you this day and always.

In His Name, BC
prae-Cristo

Bibliograpy

BOOK OF GOD, THE; the Bible as a Novel by Walter Wangerin, Jr.; Zondervan Publishing House; Grand Rapids MI; 1996.

COMPLETE PARALLEL BIBLE, THE with the Apocryphal/ Deuterocanonical Books: New Revised Standard Version, Revised English Bible, New American Bible, New Jerusalem Bible; Oxford University Press; New York & Oxford; 1993.

COTTON PATCH VERSION OF LUKE & ACTS, THE by Clarence Jordan; Association Press; New York; 1975.

FIVE BOOKS OF MOSES, THE: Genesis, Exodus, Leviticus, Numbers, and Deuteronomy; The Schocken Bible: Volume 1; a new translation with introductions, commentary, and notes by Everett Fox; Schocken Books; New York; 1995.

HOLY BIBLE, Authorized King James Version; Zondervan Publishing House; Grand Rapids MI; 1994.

HOLY BIBLE - New Revised Standard Version with Apocrypha; Oxford University Press; New York & Oxford; 1989.

JESUS BOOK, THE, an illustrated edition of The Living New Testament; Hodder and Stoughton & Coverdale House Publishers, IL; 1971.

NEW ENGLISH BIBLE, THE, with the Apocrypha; the Delegates of the Oxford University Press & the Syndics of the Cambridge University Press; 1970.

NEW INTERNATIONAL VERSION, The Living Insights Study Bible; Charles R. Swindoll, General Editor; Zondervan Publishing House; Grand Rapids MI; 1996.

NEW TESTAMENT OCTAPLA, THE, eight English Versions of the New Testament in the Tyndale-King James Tradition: Tyndale (1525), Great Bible (1539), Geneva Bible (1560), Bishops' Bible (1568), Rheims (1582), King James (1611), RV and ASV (1881), Revised Standard Version (1946); edited by Luther A. Weigle; Thomas Nelson & Sons; New York; 1951.

PSALMS/NOW by Leslie F. Brandt; Concordia Publishing House, St. Louis MO; 1973.

READER'S DIGEST BIBLE, THE, condensed from the Revised Standard Version, Old & New Testaments; Bruce M. Metzger, General Editor; The Reader's Digest Association; Pleasantville, New York; 1982.

Visit **www.bccrothersauthor.com** to know more about the author and buy her books.

Be A Better Person is available on Amazon and other online bookstores.